HIRING LIBRARY EMPLOYEES

A How-To-Do-It Manual

RICHARD E. RUBIN

HOW-TO-DO-IT MANUALS
FOR LIBRARIES

Number 37

NEAL-SCHUMAN PUBLISHERS, INC.
New York, London

Published by Neal-Schuman Publishers, Inc.
100 Varick Street
New York, NY 10013

Copyright © 1993 by Richard E. Rubin

Printed and bound in the United States of America

Library of Congress Cataloging-in-Publication Data

Rubin, Richard, 1949-
    Hiring library employees : a how-to-do-it manual / Richard E.
Rubin.
        p.   cm. -- (How-to-do-it manuals for libraries ; no. 37)
    Includes bibliographical references and index.
    ISBN 1-55570-159-0
    1. Library employees--Selection and appointment--United Sates.
    I. Title   II. Series.
Z682.2.U5R83   1993
023'.9--dc20   93-36114
                                                        CIP

CONTENTS

PREFACE

Although there are several books on personnel management for librarians, there are few monographs that deal directly with the subject of hiring library staff. *Hiring Library Employees: A How-To-Do-It Manual* is intended to be a practical, rather than theoretical, guide to securing qualified employees for library service. The discussion is divided into seven sections: chapter 1 introduces the topic, identifying the areas that should be considered in developing a hiring process and touching upon the ethical obligations that employers have whenever they hire. Chapter 2 deals with the inevitable legal issues that affect hiring policies and procedures, except for the Americans with Disabilities Act which is dealt with separately at the end of the book. Chapter 3 discusses the prerequisites of the hiring process, including the policies and practices that must be in place before an employer should attempt to hire for a particular position. Chapter 4 reviews the importance of and techniques for effective recruitment of library staff, including minority recruitment. Chapter 5 is a detailed discussion of how to implement a hiring process in 21 steps. Chapter 6 confronts the often neglected issue of training and orientation of new workers. Chapter 7 specifically discusses the implications of the 1990 Americans with Disabilities Act, with special attention to the guidelines established by the Federal Equal Employment Opportunity Commission. A brief concluding chapter summarizes the factors that should be considered by an employer when developing and implementing a hiring policy. Among the appendixes are sample policies and forms, and a copy of the *Uniform Guidelines on Employee Selection Procedures* from the Federal Register. These guidelines serve as an important foundation when assessing whether specific hiring policies or practices violate the civil rights of applicants. Because there is some overlap with the author's more general book on personnel work, *Human Resource Management in Libraries: Theory and Practice* (Neal-Schuman, 1990), some sections of the earlier work have been incorporated into the present text.

The author would like to acknowledge the cooperation of the Akron-Summit (Ohio) County Public Library, the Lexington (Kentucky) Public Library, and the Cleveland Area Metropolitan (Ohio) Library System, for their willingness to allow some of their forms and policies to be reprinted in this book.

1 INTRODUCTION

Hiring is the single most important decision that an employer makes. No decision has greater consequences for the organization or is more fraught with pitfalls. When selecting employees, one is confronted with a perplexing variety of institutional, legal, philosophical, psychological and social constraints. The hiring decision is especially important for libraries because employee turnover rates are relatively low especially among degreed librarians. This means that there are relatively few opportunities to select employees; each decision is critical.

Unfortunately, libraries, as a rule, take little time and devote few energies and resources to the hiring process. The propensity to find convenient rather than appropriate reasons for making job selections is common. This undue haste is caused by the need to hire someone as quickly as possible so that work routines can be completed; the lack of time available to managers and administrators due to other pressing duties; the small amount of money available for the recruitment and hiring process; the need to quickly appease other staff who may be forced to take on extra duties during the vacancy.

Consider some of the more common problematic reasons one is likely to hear as a reason for selection:

"I like this person."
"The individual has lived in this community for years."
"The individual is a good friend so I can trust her."
"The rest of the staff will be happy."
"Everyone expects this individual to get the job."
"I might be sued if I don't hire him."
"The individual expects to be hired."
"I will lose this person as a friend if I don't hire her."
"The staff will be angry with me if I don't hire this person."
"I don't have a reason *not* to hire him."
"The person is prominent in the community."
"The person knows people who are prominent in the community."
"The person's brother (mother, father, sister) works here."

While these are not necessarily reasons to reject a candidate for a job, and not all are irrelevant to the hiring decision, they should still play a secondary or tertiary role in the process. Those who make personnel decisions must attend to the proper goal of hiring: to select the individual who will do an excellent job for the organization. It is the employer's responsibility to hire the individual who will be the most productive worker.

There is no magic formula for hiring the right person, but there are methods that improve the chances for a sound and defensible selection. Despite the pressures on employers to hire quickly, this temptation must be avoided in favor of a systematic and deliberate process to locate the best candidate. This manual is intended to identify and discuss the issues and methods that affect the hiring process, and improve the chances for making the best choice.

THE EFFECTS OF HIRING

For the purposes of this book, hiring is, in the broadest sense, a selection for any position. It can be a new employee entering the organization, or the placement of an employee in a position as a result of transfer, promotion, or demotion. Each decision can have serious positive or negative implications for the organization. Consider what hiring the right employee can do for your library.

Good employees are:

- Cooperative and pleasant to work with
- Satisfied by getting the job done well
- Hard-working and desire challenges
- Likely to focus on the positive aspects of the workplace rather than problems
- Willing to offer creative ideas and novel solutions to problems
- Willing to "go the extra mile" when the library requires extra effort
- Good recruitment sources themselves because they are likely to know individuals who are like themselves
- Good models for other employees; good employees serve as examples, especially for new workers

- Good sources for promotion as openings with greater responsibility arise.

In addition, the organization benefits in many other ways including:

- Reduced supervisory time: supervisors need not spend extra time observing, training, and documenting the person's work.
- Reduced administrative time dealing with performance problems: administrators can spend time planning services rather than dealing with performance problems.
- Less stress on performance evaluation: supervisors need not spend time on documenting poor performance and developing plans for improvement; employees need not dread the tensions and potential conflicts that arise from poor performance evaluations.
- Reduced employee turnover: job satisfaction is closely correlated with employee turnover. When employees are well matched to their jobs the chances are much better that they will be satisfied workers.
- Good public relations: there is a much greater chance the public will be satisfied with good employees and have a positive image of the library.

None of these advantages accrue when the employer hires the wrong individual. On the contrary, when a poor performer is hired, the organization expends its time and energies in nonproductive efforts, including:

- Disciplining the individual through oral and written warnings, disciplinary hearings, and suspensions.
- Spending extra time supervising the individual, checking work, and providing additional training.
- Protecting against legal liabilities by ensuring that all actions concerning the employee are lawful by consultation with lawyers and other administrators.
- Defending actions taken by the employee in grievance procedures, courts, or administrative agencies such as the Office of Equal Employment Opportunity.

- Pacifying and motivating unhappy staff members who are adversely affected by the poor performance of the employee.
- Pacifying unhappy patrons who are victimized by the attitude or incompetence of the poor performer.

Experienced library managers and administrators are well aware of the impact that a single poor performing employee can have not only on the individuals who work closely with the poor performer, but on the social relations, morale, and productivity of the entire organization.

CRITICAL ELEMENTS IN THE HIRING PROCESS

Because of the importance of hiring, it is necessary to see the process in systematic terms. Among the critical elements in this process are:

Established policies and procedures: It is essential that clearly written policies, procedures and forms be established prior to beginning the hiring process. Failure to do so could result in serious legal liabilities.

Effective recruitment techniques and strategies: The organization must have an effective method to identify talented individuals who could perform the job well. This involves locating sources of potential employees, posting and advertising positions, and taking applications.

The use of job analysis to determine the nature of the job to be filled: Before hiring for a position it is necessary to understand what the job actually is. Otherwise, it is easy to hire the wrong individual.

Identification of qualified candidates: The most difficult part of hiring is obtaining all the necessary and relevant information to make an informed selection. Applications and other job related information must be evaluated so that interviewees can be selected.

Effective interview procedures and techniques: The employer must be able to develop questions and other techniques to determine the suitability of the candidate.

Reference checking: The employer must develop techniques that will elicit desired information from previous employers to determine if the candidate's knowledge, skills, and abilities match those needed in the position.

Selection of successful candidate: After all the information has been collected, a judgment must be made regarding the best qualified candidate. A job offer must then be made and unsuccessful candidates informed.

Records maintenance: Various records must be kept, evaluated, and stored to ensure that the hire is lawful. The employer must be particularly scrupulous that the hiring practices of the organization does not disproportionately screen out members of minority and other protected groups.

New employee orientation and training: The hiring process is not over until the new employee is adequately familiar with the job and the organization.

The hiring process is a considerable undertaking and requires cooperation among administrators, managers, supervisors, and staff. The rewards for effective hiring are great as are the penalties when mistakes are made.

ETHICAL CONSIDERATIONS IN THE HIRING PROCESS

The hiring situation is one in which people are being evaluated and a great deal of personal information is being collected. It is also a situation of considerable inequity—the employer holds all or most of the power and the candidate must respond to the employer's demands if he or she expects to compete with other candidates. Under such circumstances, it is the employer's ethical burden to treat applicants fairly and honestly. The library profession recognizes the ethics implicit in human resource management in the *ALA Code of Ethics* which states in part:

> Librarians must adhere to the principles of due process and equality of opportunity in peer relationships and personnel actions.[1]

What are some of the ethical responsibilities of an employer who hires?

The obligation to be truthful: The employer should communicate the nature and responsibilities of a job opening accurately including potential salaries, benefits, job tasks, and opportunities for advancement. Obviously, the employer is under no obligation to discuss matters unrelated to the job or to divulge information that is confidential, but the employer should not withhold pertinent information nor distort information.

The obligation to protect privacy and not to invade it: As a rule, information gained during the hiring process should be treated as confidential, which means that only individuals who need to know should be provided with the relevant information. It is the obligation of the employer not to probe into areas of an individual's life that are unrelated to the ability to perform the job. This is an abuse of the power relationship which forces candidates to reveal inappropriate information simply because the employer asks for it. The notion of privacy also extends to respecting a candidate's wish not to inform a current employer of the candidate's application until an appropriate time.

The obligation to treat all candidates fairly: No matter what the law requires, it is the obligation of the employer to create a hiring process that provides equal access and opportunity for the job; each applicant should be treated fairly in regard to gathering similar information and evaluating it with similar criteria. No candidate should be given an advantage; all candidates should be given an equal opportunity for the job.

The obligation to hire the best individual for the job: The duty of the selector is not just to the candidate but to the organization as a whole. The obligation of the selector is to choose the individual who will best serve and advance the interest of the organization. The self-interest of the selector, or the interest of the few, must be subjugated to the interest of the organization. Common ethical conflicts arise, for example, when an applicant is a friend of the selector. The selection decision must be based on which candidate will work the hardest and perform the best and it is unethical to select candidates merely because their friendship would make the workplace more pleasant and beneficial for the selector.

REFERENCES

1. American Library Association, *Code of Ethics*, Chicago: ALA.

2 LEGAL CONSIDERATIONS

It is impossible to deal with the subject of hiring without reviewing some of the important legal considerations. The employer must be especially diligent because the penalties for violating the law can be very expensive. In addition, the current litigious climate makes it essential that *all* staff members involved in the hiring process be aware of legal obligations and pitfalls. In some situations several individuals may come into contact with the candidate in what seems to be informal circumstances, but for the purposes of hiring, no circumstance should be considered informal. This means that if the candidate is introduced to members of a department, or if employees are invited to dine or meet with the candidate, inappropriate questions, comments, or behavior on the part of employees, even when innocent, could subject the employer to legal liabilities. The employer is responsible for exercising control over such situations. Below is a brief description of some of the major legal concerns. This section is not intended to be comprehensive or to serve as a substitute for legal advice. Employers must consult legal counsel in the development of hiring policies, procedures, and practices, and whenever there are questions concerning the legality of the hiring practices and decisions.

FEDERAL CIVIL RIGHTS ACTS

A variety of civil rights acts have been passed by the Federal government since 1866 to prohibit discrimination against various groups. These include the Civil Rights Acts of 1866, 1871, 1964, 1972 and 1991, the Rehabilitation Act of 1973, the Age Discrimination in Employment Act, the Equal Pay Act, and most recently the Americans with Disabilities Act (ADA). The ADA may have substantial implications for library employers and is treated separately in Chapter 7.

Each of these anti-discrimination laws have their own unique features, but when taken as a whole there are certain generalizations in terms of hiring that are useful for the employer to keep in mind:

1. It is unlawful for an employer to refuse to hire an individual on the basis of his or her race, creed, color,

national origin, sex (including whether she is pregnant), or disability.

2. Questions during the hiring and interview process concerning race, national origin, sex, and disability should be strictly avoided.

3. Generally, discriminatory *intent* does *not* have to be shown for an employer to be found guilty of discrimination. That is, so long as an individual can show that the employer used an unlawful consideration or criterion as part of the hiring decision, the organization may be culpable.

4. An employer may be found to discriminate if it can be shown that its practices (regardless of intent to discriminate) have the effect of disproportionately screening out groups protected by the law. This is called "disparate impact" or "adverse impact." These practices may seem quite harmless, such as requiring a college degree, or administering a job test, but if the effect is to screen out members of certain groups, then the employer must justify the criterion or practice as a business necessity, and that there are no other alternative procedures that would eliminate the adverse impact.

5. It is unlawful to offer different rates of pay to men and women in so far as the job requires equal skill, effort, responsibility, and has similar working conditions (Equal Pay Act). There are exceptions to this requirement, although the exceptions generally deal with payment after the individual has been working and that result from differences in tenure or work performance. Specifically, exceptions can be made if there is an established merit system, seniority system, if the payment of wages is based on quantity or quality of production, or if the criteria used to pay differently is not based on sex. As a rule, however, when hiring males and females into similar positions (e.g., starting reference librarians), starting pay rates should be equal.

6. It is unlawful to make hiring decisions based on stereotypes about women's ability to perform job functions. One cannot assume, for example, that women will have higher turnover rates because they are married or

have a family, that women cannot lift heavy objects, or that they are unable to perform management functions.

7. It is unlawful to suggest or require that a candidate provide sexual favors as a condition for a favorable hiring decision, or to subject a candidate to sexual innuendos or sexual advances. The issue of sexual harassment has become especially prominent since the Supreme Court hearings of Justice Clarence Thomas. This type of unlawful conduct is clearly a matter of concern in librarianship in which more than 75 percent of the workforce is female and a disproportionate number of administrators are male.

The groups that are usually protected by civil rights legislation are called "protected classes." They consist of African-Americans, Hispanics, American Indians, Asians, veterans, individuals with disabilities, individuals over 40 years of age, and women. These groups have been singled out for protection, because they have historically suffered from employment discrimination. Usually, but not always, it is the U.S. Equal Employment Opportunity Commission and/or State Human Rights Commissions that process claims of discrimination prior to cases actually going to court. If the employer goes to court and loses, penalties for violating the discrimination laws vary based in part on the seriousness of the offense and which law is violated. Nonetheless the loss of a civil rights case can prove quite expensive to the organization. In some cases, such as in sexual harassment, individual employees may also bear a personal liability.

Individual states may have civil rights laws that parallel the content of the federal legislation, and some local areas may even have their own civil rights legislation which extends civil rights protection beyond those protected by federal or state law, such as legislation barring discrimination based on sexual preference. Individuals who believe their civil rights have been violated by an employer may file civil rights complaints using federal, state, and/or local laws.

In addition to the anti-discrimination laws, there are also a variety of guidelines which are promulgated by the federal government and to which employers are expected to adhere. These guidelines are usually prepared by the Equal Employment Opportunity Commission (EEOC). There are, for example, separate guidelines for sex discrimination, including sexual harassment and pregnancy discrimination guidelines, and guidelines for discrimination on the basis of age, religion and disability. The EEOC has also developed additional guidelines related to the hiring process, most notably, the "Uniform Guidelines on Employee Selection Procedures" (see Appendix A). These guidelines should be reviewed by employers beginning the hiring process.

THE CONCEPT OF DISCRIMINATION

Employers must be cognizant of the nature of discrimination in the workplace, especially the manner in which discrimination may be perceived by state and executive civil rights agencies such as the Equal Employment Opportunity Commission (EEOC). There are two basic types of discrimination: discrimination that results from disparate treatment and that which results from disparate impact.

DISPARATE TREATMENT

According to the EEOC, disparate treatment occurs "where members of a race, sex, or ethnic groups have been denied the same employment, promotion, membership, or other employment opportunities as have been available to other employees or applicants."[1] In essence, disparate treatment means that individuals who are members of protected classes are treated differently than individuals who are not members of protected classes. Examples of disparate treatment in the hiring process would be the following:

- If a more stringent selection criteria were applied to a minority candidate.
- If female candidates were asked to take additional job tests.
- If older candidates were asked to provide a different number of job references.
- If different application procedures were required of minority candidates.

It is not difficult for a candidate to establish a *prima facia* case of discrimination. The Supreme Court in *McDonnell Douglas Corporation* v. *Green* noted that the individual had to show:

1. That they belonged to a racial minority.
2. That they applied and were qualified for a job for which the employer was seeking applicants.
3. That, despite qualifications, they were rejected.
4. That after his rejection, the position remained open and the employer continued to seek applicants of complainant's qualifications.[2]

Other similar conditions could also meet the standards of a *prima facia* case. For example, the case could be made by any member of a protected class, not just a racial minority, and the employer may have selected another candidate and not just continued the search. It is not necessary for the complainant to prove intent. Once a *prima facia* case has been established, the employer must "articulate some legitimate nondiscriminatory reason for the employee's rejection."[3] This highlights the need for the employer to have a systematic process that can identify legitimate business reasons for selecting employees. Once the employer provides a legitimate business reason, the burden of proof again shifts to the complainant who must show that the reason given by the employer is a pretext for discrimination.[4] The best way for an employer to demonstrate that the reasons for hire are not a pretext is to have truthful and good reasons for the selection.

ADVERSE IMPACT

Adverse impact deals with the discriminatory effects of employments practices, including hiring practices, in contrast to acts directed against specific individuals. The *Uniform Guidelines on Employee Selection Procedures* states that:

> . . . a selection process which has an adverse impact on the employment opportunities of members of a race, color, religion, sex, or national origin group . . . and thus disproportionately screens them out is unlawfully discriminatory unless the process or its component

procedures have been validated in accord with the Guidelines . . .[5]

Any hiring practice that might work against a protected class could be subject to challenge, even if the practice appears to be neutral. This would include any procedures, job tests, or job requirements. If any practice operates to exclude members of a protected class, it must be shown to be job-related, a business necessity, and that there is no alternative practice that could be instituted which had no adverse impact.

How does an employer determine if adverse impact is occurring in the hiring process? The *Uniform Guidelines on Employee Selection Procedures* suggests a four-step process to determine adverse impact using what is sometimes referred to as the "four-fifths" rule:

1. Calculate the rate of selection for each group (divide the number of persons selected from a group by the number of applicants from that group). A group can be defined as any member of an "affected [protected] class" such as blacks, individuals of Hispanic origin, handicapped people, or females.

2. Observe which group has the highest selection rate;

3. Calculate the impact ratios, by comparing the selection rate for each group with that of the highest group (divide the selection rate for a group by the selection rate for the highest group).

4. Observe whether the selection rate for any group is substantially less (i.e., usually less than 4/5ths or 80%) than the selection rate for the highest group. If it is, adverse impact is indicated in most circumstances.[6]

In the case below provided by the EEOC, the organization is evaluating its hiring by comparing the rates of selection for African-American and white employees:

Applicants	Hire	Selection rate/percent
80 Whites	48	48/80 or 60%
40 Blacks	12	12/50 or 30%

Comparing the black selection rate with the white rate, the black rate is one-half of that of the white rate (30/60=50%). Because this is less than 80% (the four-fifths rule), an adverse impact has been demonstrated. The finding that there is adverse impact does not require a finding of discriminatory intent, nor does it require that the cause of the adverse impact be immediately apparent.

Employers should monitor their hiring practices annually for adverse impact. A good place to start is to determine if the overall hiring rates of protected classes and unprotected classes are similar. If there is no adverse impact, and if the organization's workforce generally reflects the composition of the outside workforce, then the employer's concerns are considerably reduced. If, on the other hand, the employer suspects that an adverse impact exists, then it is up to the employer to act to determine the cause of the adverse impact and to remedy the situation if possible.

The *Uniform Guidelines* define a variety of obligations for the employer when adverse impact is found. Among these obligations are that the employer is required to:

- Validate the hiring process. For example, if the employer uses employment tests or evaluation interviews, and these practices are found to create an adverse impact, then these tests or interviews must be validated.
- Seek out alternative practices that are valid and job-related to eliminate the adverse impact, or demonstrate that there are no other valid alternative practices that would reduce the adverse impact.[7]

Once adverse impact has been found, it is essential to examine all the aspects of the hiring process to identify which procedures have an adverse impact on candidates as they proceed through the hiring process. The conservative employer investigates possible adverse impact *before* a challenge is made to hiring practices. An employer is not required to validate an employment practice that has no adverse impact, but once adverse impact is found, a validation process is required. This process may involve the use of complex statistical and research methods which are time-consuming, expensive, and often require the hiring of a consultant. A review of these methods are published in the *Uniform Guidelines*.

AFFIRMATIVE ACTION

Affirmative action has been part of the employment process for more than 25 years. The purpose of affirmative action is to provide an opportunity to remedy the past effects of discrimination on minorities and other groups. The result of this discrimination has been a workforce largely dominated by white males, who have had access to superior education, training and promotions.

The EEOC defines affirmative action as those actions "appropriate to overcome the effects of past or present practices, policies, or other barriers to equal employment opportunity."[8] This is usually accomplished by singling out minorities and other protected classes for special recruitment and employment consideration. This practice has become quite controversial in recent times, because some individuals, who are not members of protected classes (i.e., white males), have argued that this special attention is itself a form of discrimination, and often charge "reverse discrimination." Nonetheless, affirmative action is an important social responsibility which should be implemented when necessary.

DETERMINING A NEED FOR AFFIRMATIVE ACTION

Although there are instances, such as with a court order, in which affirmative action is mandatory, most organizations have voluntary affirmative action plans. These plans usually state that the employer will not discriminate. Such plans may also include what is called a workforce analysis. The EEOC suggests that an employer conduct a "reasonable self-analysis" to determine if affirmative action is necessary in its organization. This is usually accomplished by comparing the composition of the organization's workforce with that of the workforce outside the organization. If, for example, 25 percent of the clerical workforce outside the organization is Asian, then approximately 25 percent of the clerical workforce inside the library should be Asian. When disproportionately small numbers of individuals from a protected class are represented, this is referred to as *underutilization*. In identifying the workforce composition outside the organization, it may be necessary to use information on the local, state, or national level, depending on the position. For example, for clerical workers the local city or county workforce data would be most appropriate. For professional positions or administrative ones, state or national data may be more appropriate.

When underutilization is found, the employer should create short and long-term affirmative action hiring goals with hiring targets that would create a representative workforce. These should not be construed as quotas—quotas imply that the organization is compelled to hire individuals from a particular protected class. Rather, these targets should be construed as guidelines for action. The EEOC has identified several strategies for accomplishing affirmative action goals:

- The establishment of a recruitment program to attract qualified candidates.
- Changing job selection tests or procedures which have the effect of eliminating members of protected classes.
- Developing procedures to ensure that all qualified applicants from protected classes are actively considered when positions open.
- Developing monitoring programs to measure the effectiveness of the affirmative action program, and the development of efficient means to change the program as needed.[9]

Given the sensitive legal climate in which affirmative action exists, the employer should attempt to create a plan with a clear rationale and which is as fair as possible to all concerned. Among the characteristics that a good affirmative action plan should possess are the following:

1. The plan should be tailored directly to the problems identified in the self-analysis.

2. The plan should not unnecessarily restrict opportunities for advancement or promotion for the workforce as a whole, that is, nonminorities should not be prohibited from advancing in the organization.

3. The plan should not dictate the discharge of nonminorities in order to hire members of protected groups.

4. The provisions of the plan should only be in place so long as the imbalance exists and should be discontinued when the affirmative action goals have been achieved.[10]

This last point is important for several reasons. The organization should not attempt to remedy past discriminations by over-compensating, that is, by hiring a greater percentage of minorities than is reflected in the outside laborforce. Also, it is important that the affirmative action plan established by the organization be followed by all individuals responsible for hiring. Managers or administrators should not be engaged in implementing their own personal affirmative action goals.

OTHER LEGISLATION AFFECTING EMPLOYMENT

In addition to Civil Rights legislation, there are a variety of laws which may affect the hiring process. These include the following:

Immigration Reform and Control Act of 1986: This act is intended to ensure that employees are legally able to work in the United States. The burden is placed on the employer during the hiring process to acquire the necessary documentation to substantiate the employee's ability to work.

Residence requirements: Some localities may require that an individual be a resident of the city or political jurisdiction, or it may require that the individual subsequently move into the jurisdiction within a specified period of time.

Prevailing wage statutes: Some laws require that the rate of pay be equal to the prevailing wage for similar jobs in the area. Such statutes may apply especially to positions which are funded through state or federal grants.

Maximum wage statutes: These statutes set a maximum amount that a particular position can be paid. This is most common for high level positions in government. For example, such a law might prevent a library director from being paid more than the mayor.

EMPLOYER LIABILITY AND NEGLIGENT HIRE

In addition to specific laws and regulations, there is increasing legal activity attempting to define the liabilities of an employer if the employer hires an individual who subsequently acts negligently. There are two senses of liability that should be noted. The first sense is the one most commonly understood and accepted in which liability arises from the employee's negligent acts when performing her job duties (respondent superior). With the decline in sovereign immunity for public employers, it is clear that the employer must exercise caution in hiring employees who may injure others, including fellow employees. Certain library jobs, therefore, might require special attention, such as that of bookmobile driver, or jobs involving service to the homebound or children.

The doctrine of negligent hire, however, is even broader and more complex. It suggests that an employer could be held liable for the actions of an employee which are *foreseeable* even when the employee's actions lie outside the scope of their job. As one court decision states:

> Liability for negligent hiring arises only when a particular unfitness of an applicant creates a danger of harm to a third person which the employer knows, or should have known, when he hired and placed this applicant in employment when he could injure others . . .[11]

Of particular importance to library employers is the notion of foreseeable danger, or danger which the employer should have known. Certainly many employers would act if they knew that an employee was dangerous, but to what extent is an employer obligated to check on a candidate to relieve them of the charge that they "should have known" about the employee's unfitness? The employer may, in general, be expected to exercise "reasonable care" when members of the public are involved.[12] The extent of this care increases as the vulnerability of the public increases. Again, the types of jobs involved in libraries might be those who have access to private residences (e.g., a library staff member performing "at-home" visits), a bookmobile driver, or individuals who work with children.[13]

These liabilities make it incumbent on the employer to make thorough reference checks, make sure that the job knowledge and skills of a position are clear, and that the individual hired possesses that knowledge and skill.

REFERENCES

1. *Uniform Guidelines on Employee Selection Procedures, Part 1607*, CFR29 Ch. XIV:1607.11.

2. *McDonnell Douglas Corporation v. Green*, 411 U.S. 792 (1973).

3. *McDonnell Douglas v. Green*: 802.

4. *McDonnell Douglas v. Green*: 804.

5. *Uniform Guidelines*, 11997.

6. *Uniform Guidelines*, 11998.

7. *Uniform Guidelines*, Section 1607.3.

8. *Code of Federal Regulations*, "Part 1608-Affirmative Action Appropriate Under Title VII of the Civil Rights Act of 1963, As Amended," 29 CFR Part 1608:238.

9. *Code of Federal Regulations*, "Part 1607-Uniform Guidelines of Employee Selection Procedures," 29 CFR Ch XIV:235-236.

10. Kahn, Steven C., Barbara A. Brown, and Brent E. Zepke, *Personnel Director's Legal Guide: 1988 Cumulative Supplement*: S6-30; and *Code of Federal Regulations*, "Part 1608 . . ." 29 CFR Part 1608: 241.

11. *Fallon v. Indian Trail School*, 500 N.E. 2d 101 (Ill. App 2 Dist. 1986) as cited in Anne Marie Ryan and Marja Lasek, "Negligent Hiring and Defamation: Areas of Liability Related to Pre-Employment Inquiries," *Personnel Psychology* 44 (1991): 293-319.

12. Ryan and Lasek, pp. 298-299.

13. Ryan and Lasek, pp. 302-303.

3 PREREQUISITES TO THE HIRING PROCESS

HIRING POLICIES

All institutions should have policies and procedures that create an orderly and consistent hiring process. As part of the commitment to sound employment practices, libraries should have these policies clearly delineated in an employment handbook (see Appendix B). If there is a collective bargaining agreement, these policies may be enunciated in the contract. As a rule, the policies affecting hiring might include:

1. A general statement committing the library to non-discrimination in employment and affirmative action and a warning to violators that severe penalties for discrimination will be imposed.

2. A statement regarding how job openings are advertised within the library. Some libraries advertise such openings a set number of days before the job is posted outside the library; in other cases, an internal posting may be the only evidence of any opening unless there are no satisfactory internal candidates. Although it may be useful for morale on some occasions to promote from within, employers should be careful not to commit themselves to such a policy unless they have a sound internal development program which is sure to produce an excellent candidate. Remember that promoting the wrong person from inside can do as much or more damage to morale over time.

3. A statement regarding who is responsible for filling positions and who sets the salary of employees. In most libraries, the ultimate responsibility for both rests with the board of trustees, but whatever or whoever is responsible, this should be noted.

4. A statement on the basic criteria for selection. Generally, seniority should be avoided as a criteria because it is not, in and of itself, a predictor of job success. Issues such as education, technical and professional background, as well as the intellectual and personal qualifications of the candidate might be noted. Personal qualifications may include ability to cooperate and work productively with staff and the public.

5. A statement regarding nepotism. For example, an employer might note that the library would not hire an applicant if his or her employment would place him under the director supervision of an immediate family member, or would place her as a supervisor of an immediate family member.

6. A statement of job commitment. The employer might designate a length of time (e.g., one year) during which the employee is expected to remain with the organization. The employer must be very careful, however, not to create the impression that the employee must remain with the library for that period. Such a statement might be construed as an implied contract and make it very difficult for the library to terminate the employee if needed.

7. A statement regarding the employment status of the individual at the time of hire. It is essential that the employer establish clearly under what conditions the employee has been hired. Two common conditions are probationary status and employment at will.

Probationary status: Traditionally, libraries have referred to new hires as "probationary employees." This implies that there is a short time, perhaps three months to a year, in which the employee is on a trial status. During this time, the employee can be treated differently from regular employees. She may receive few or no benefits, she may receive more frequent performance evaluations, and, perhaps most important, she could be terminated with little or no cause. Once an employee passes the probationary period, many libraries consider her a permanent employee unless her performance or behavior warrants disciplinary action. The use of probationary status however, is not generally recommended today because it implies a commitment to continued employment unless a good cause is shown otherwise once the probation period is over. Although, on the face of it this seems only fair, what the employer sees as good cause may not be the same for what a jury sees as good cause. Hence, using a probationary status may increase the legal liabilities of a library and may significantly reduce administrative discretion. As a result, there is a movement to use another doctrine called employment at will.

Employment at will: The employment at will doctrine is actually a very old one in our judicial system. It holds that the relationship between employee and employer is a voluntary one and that it may be terminated at any time by either party. Essentially, the doctrine holds that an employer, in the absence of a written contract, may terminate an employee for good cause, bad cause, or no cause at all. Such a doctrine is still used as an employer's defense, although it has been significantly eroded by a variety of laws intended to protect employees from discriminatory and arbitrary actions on the part of employers. Nonetheless, such a policy obviously gives an employer the greatest latitude in exercising judgement regarding an employee's suitability for continued employment. In selecting such a policy, the library should make clear exactly what this means: that the employee could be asked to leave for no reason whatsoever subject to whatever provisions there are for advanced notice (see Appendix C). Employers who currently are operating under a different doctrine such as probationary status *should consult with competent legal counsel if they wish to change the conditions of employment.*

8. In addition, there should be a statement about how one applies for promotions and transfers. In many ways this can be considered just another aspect of hiring an individual for a position, the difference being that the individual is currently employed in another position within the organization. Among the issues to be explored in these policies are how announcements for vacancies are made, the procedure to apply for a promotion or transfer, the length of time an employee must be in her current position before application can be made, to whom applications are made, and a basic criteria for promotion or transfer (e.g., promise of future development, education and technical background, and personal qualifications). A statement should also be made concerning how pay rates are set. As with the regular hiring process, the status of a

newly transferred or promoted individual should be stated clearly (e.g., is she on probation?).

APPLICATION MATERIALS

All application materials serve two basic purposes. First, to provide information to the employer regarding the knowledge, skill, and ability of the applicant. All forms must be designed to secure the necessary job-related information in an orderly fashion. The second function is public relations. Application materials convey an attitude or organizational philosophy to the applicant. Sloppy and unclear materials communicate that the organization does not care or is unprofessional. Well prepared materials suggest that the organization is professional and concerned. It is an inevitable fact that only one of many applicants successfully secures a given position. Those applicants who are unsuccessful are especially vulnerable to negative feelings. Producing materials that are clear, well-organized, and professional improves (albeit does not guarantee) the chances that applicants will be positively disposed to the organization regardless of the outcome.

THE APPLICATION FORM

The most common way to obtain information about a job applicant is through the application form (Appendix D). It is very important that the employer use a form prepared by the library and not simply use a resume for application information. There are several reasons for this. First, resumes provide information in the manner in which the candidate wants to provide it. Resumes can omit important information. An application ensures that all information deemed pertinent by the library is collected. Second, the employer can collect the pertinent information in a consistent order. Specific information is found in the same place on the application form, which makes comparison of candidates much easier. Third, the application form usually contains an agreement attesting to the truth and completeness of the information provided thereon. This may allow the employer to take subsequent action if falsification is found.

The order of obtaining information may vary but the application should at least include the following:

Name and logo of institution (if any): This should be prominently displayed and aesthetically appealing as it is a means of communicating pride in the organization.

Statement of EEO policy: This is an opportunity for the organization to demonstrate its commitment to social responsibility and fairness.

Date of application: This is especially useful when weeding applications as they become out-of-date.

Name, address, social security number, phone number: This type of information is essential for communicating with an applicant and sometimes useful for reference and identification purposes.

Inquiry concerning age if under 18: Although it is not appropriate to ask the age of the applicant or the birth date, many states have laws related to the employment of individuals under the age of 18. These laws may restrict the number of consecutive hours worked or when an individual may work (e.g., evening work). For this reason, it is appropriate to explore if the individual is a minor.

Inquiry concerning U.S. citizenship or legal alien status: Because it is unlawful to hire an individual who cannot lawfully work in the United States and the law places the burden on the employer to ensure that the individual is so qualified, it is appropriate to make this inquiry. Note that this is not the same as inquiring into an individual's nationality or ancestry, which is still prohibited.

Inquiry into preferences for full- or part-time employment or job sharing: In order to match the right job with the right individual, it is very useful to know what type of work schedule the applicant desires. Individuals, for example, seeking full-time work are not likely to remain in a part-time opening for long. Unless the organization anticipates a full-time opening in the near future, hiring such individuals may be an invitation to employee dissatisfaction and turnover.

Inquiry into preferences for evening and weekend work:
Library work, especially public services, often requires that employees work evenings and weekends. For this reason, it is important to know if the applicant has a sufficiently flexible schedule. The employer must be careful, however, to avoid probing religious backgrounds. Applicants who indicate that they are unable to work certain times for religious reasons may require accommodation and should not be rejected out of hand before exploring the options available under EEO guidelines.

Inquiries into professional, business, civic, volunteer activities, and offices (omitting those that would indicate race, color, religion, sex, national origin, age or disability): It is not uncommon, especially for women, that their work experience was interrupted by the raising of a family. During this period, women often demonstrate leadership, managerial, and organizational abilities through participation in voluntary organizations. Consequently, it is especially important, given the numerical dominance of women in libraries, to explore non-workplace activities. One difficult aspect of this query is that the names of many clubs and organizations reveal information such as religion, national origin or race.

Inquiry into military service: Many individuals with limited formal education receive relevant training and education while serving in the military. The applicant should be given the opportunity to provide this information on the application form.

Inquiry into any felony convictions including date and type of felony: It is the responsibility of the employer to protect staff, the public, fiscal, and physical resources of the organization. Individuals who may have a propensity to commit unlawful acts should be identified. The commission of a felony, however, should not, in and of itself, exclude an applicant. After all, once a debt to society has been paid, an individual should have a chance to succeed. The type of crime committed may have a bearing. For example, it would be unwise to hire an individual who was convicted of fraud or embezzlement for a position that handles monies; similarly an individual who has been convicted for molestation or rape would seem inappropriate in an organization with many women or children.

Inquiry into the types of jobs which interest the individual:
In organizations with many different types of jobs, it may be useful to indicate some of the basic types of jobs available (e.g., library assistant, clerical, secretary, librarian, graphic artist, or maintenance and janitorial). This is especially useful in organizations that take applications even when no specific opening is available. This question allows individuals to "self-select" positions for which they think they are qualified.

Inquiries into education and training: Educational background is considered an important part of assessing the abilities of a candidate. The applicant should provide the name of each educational institution attended, when and if graduation occurred, major subjects studied, and grade point average.

Inquiries into other skills: In some cases, individuals may have received skills and training in vocational or training programs not associated with formal educational institutions, for example from the Urban League. Applicants should be given the opportunity to reveal this training.

Inquiries into employment history: The work background of an applicant provides the single most important source of information on predicting job success. Among the items to be explored are (a) the name and address of employer, (b) title of last position, (c) duties, (d) supervisor's name, (e) reason for leaving, (f) dates of employment, and (g) rate of pay when leaving. In addition, for each position, the employee should be asked if the employer can be contacted for a reference. Although granting permission to obtain references is usually part of agreement signed at the end of an application, it is useful to get agreement for each job; that is, a space should be provided by each position for the applicant to indicate agreement to get a reference. In this way, the employer can determine if the employee is reluctant about specific positions, and if so, the employer may subsequently inquire about this reluctance in any interview if the applicant gets to this part of the hiring process.

The application agreement: The end of the application form should contain an agreement which the applicant must sign and date. The agreement should include the following: (a) certification that the statements made on the application form are truthful and complete, (b) authorization of any investigation necessary to determine the suitability of the candidate, (c) a release from liability for any referees who provide information about the candidate, (d) a warning that falsification can lead to termination, and (e) an agreement to abide by all rules of the institution if employed. In addition, if the employer hires "at-will," a statement indicating the meaning of "at-will" employment, (i.e., that the employee may be released for any cause or no cause) may be included. Below this statement should be space for the applicant's signature and date.

PRE-EMPLOYMENT INQUIRY FORM

Among the other forms used during application is the pre-employment inquiry form (Appendix D). This is used to maintain a record of individuals who apply who are members of protected classes. The form itself gathers information that is otherwise prohibited by law including race, gender, age, status as a veteran, and disability. Completion of the form is voluntary and the information contained should be stored *in a separate location from the application form*. It should not be viewed by individuals involved in the hiring process unless its consultation involves encouraging the hiring of a minority under a *bona fide* affirmative action plan.

REFERENCE FORMS TO PREVIOUS OR CURRENT EMPLOYER

Another form used during the application process is the form for checking references. The form may consist of a checklist of traits and questions concerning the candidate's knowledge, skills, and ability, or it may simply provide a space onto which a narrative account of the employee's abilities would be written. The type of information that should be on the reference form is discussed in Chapter 5.

OTHER HIRING FORMS

Employers may also have a variety of point-of-hire forms. These would include all relevant, federal, state and local tax forms, insurance forms, retirement and pension plans, and the I-9 form which must be completed to confirm that the employee may lawfully work in the United States.

APPLICATION PROCEDURES

The organization should have an orderly process for the intake of applications and screening interviews if employed. It is up to each organization to determine the times at which applications will be taken. Because most libraries are public employers, it is good public relations to extend generous hours. If the library is quite small and there are few openings, it might be desirable to take applications only when positions open; this way the members of the public are not deceived into thinking jobs are readily available. Fairness and good public relations should guide the organization's decision on this matter. Whether applicants appear in person or send a letter, they should receive the same information regarding how to file an application and with whom to file the application. Also, if general screening interviews are conducted, regardless of whether openings exist, all applicants should be informed when such interviews are conducted.

Procedures for application to positions for internal applicants should also be established. These procedures should be noted in writing in an employee handbook. Procedures for applying for particular positions should also be noted in the job posting.

Additional procedures include file maintenance and access to applications. Rules should be established regarding where files are maintained, who has access to job application materials and who controls access. Access should be restricted only to those on a need-to-know basis. Because library applications become outdated fairly quickly, procedures should also be established for the timely weeding of applications.

TRAINING PROGRAMS AND MATERIALS FOR SELECTORS

There are two major reasons why training in hiring is particularly important: first, there is evidence that such training actually improves the quality of the selection; second, it decreases the chance that unlawful considerations will occur during the hiring process. As part of the training process, the employer should set aside a block of time (or blocks of time) to ensure that all individuals involved in the hiring process are sufficiently familiar with hiring policies, procedures, and techniques. In addition, employees with hiring responsibilities should be given instruction how to train new employees. Training materials should be prepared carefully, reflecting the importance the organization places on this process. Similarly, the employer must select a trainer who is knowledgeable, concerned, and committed, and who possesses strong teaching and communication skills.

Workshop sessions and written materials should include:

1. Discussion of samples of all hiring forms used in the hiring process.

2. Discussion of all hiring policies adopted by the library with special emphasis on policies regarding non-discrimination in employment and the consequences for violating such policies.

3. Discussion of all pertinent federal, state, and local laws, and regulations and guidelines pertaining to hiring. Have examples of important sections of the laws.

4. Discussion of how to evaluate resumes and job applications.

5. Discussion of how to interview effectively and on how to evaluate an interview (include a list of questions that should not be asked during an interview).

6. Discussion of how to conduct and evaluate work references.

7. Discussion of who makes final hiring decisions.

8. Discussion of the procedures for making job offers.

9. Discussion of the follow-up and orientation procedures to follow after a hiring decision is made and the employee begins to work.

JOB DESCRIPTIONS

As noted above, a critical part of the hiring process is the matching of a particular individual with a particular job. Understanding the precise nature of the job requires a clearly written, complete, and up-to-date job description. The manner in which job descriptions are prepared and written fall outside the scope of this book, but the job description, when prepared well, can serve many valuable purposes in the hiring process. Among them are the following:

- It serves as a source of information for recruitment and for preparation of job advertisements.
- It serves as a consistent source of information for evaluators concerning the job content and the required and preferred knowledge, skill, and abilities needed to perform the job.
- It serves as a source of communication to prospective applicants and interviewees who want to know about the job content.
- It serves as a source of information for job referees.
- It serves as documentation in support of a job hire if the selection decision is questioned.
- When prepared well, it sends a message to prospective employees that the organization is run professionally.

The employer must be careful that the description is complete and current, and that job selectors understand the importance of evaluating candidates based on important rather than minor job functions and responsibilities identified in the description.

WAGE AND SALARY POLICIES AND PRACTICES

Employers should have sound pay rules and policies in place when new employees are hired or employees are promoted or transferred to new positions. These rules may differ depending on the philosophy of the organization, the ease of recruiting new employees, and monetary resources of the library. Among the issues that should be addressed are the following:

1. Are new employees, who have never worked in the library before, always placed at the entry level pay for that position?

2. How are employees who are promoted to a position at a higher grade handled if the entry level for the higher grade is below the current pay rate of the employee?

3. Are new employees who serve a "probationary" period paid at a different rate than those who pass probation?

4. When employees are rehired after a break in their service to a position similar to the one they previously held, what is their rate of pay?

5. At what point do new employees begin earning benefits such as sick and vacation time? When are they eligible for hospitalization benefits?

The larger the organization and the greater the employee turnover, the more likely the employer will encounter these and other situations involving pay and benefits. Well developed and clear policies that are consistently applied will serve the employer well. All employers should be especially sensitive to the assignment of pay rates of new employees of different sexes. Employers should never, for example, hire a man at a different pay rate because men are considered the "bread winner," or because the man is more likely to leave if he doesn't get more money, or because women are more likely to leave to get married and raise a family. Such practices may well create legal liabilities for the employer.

PHYSICAL SPACE

It may seem odd to mention physical space as a prerequisite to good hiring, but it is important that the employer try to provide pleasant and private surroundings in which to conduct the hiring process. Although this is not always possible, areas for the completion of applications, interviewing, and decision-making should be as pleasant, quiet, and private as possible. Not only do such surroundings increase the chance for sound information gathering and deliberation, but it also is a public relations statement that the organization respects and cares about the prospective employee.

EEO MONITORING

It is essential that the employer carefully monitor each individual hire and the hiring process overall to ensure that employment discrimination is not occurring. This is accomplished in several ways:

1. By reviewing the pre-employment inquiry forms that are completed at the time of application. Routinely, perhaps annually, a demographic breakdown of job applicants should be prepared. This is to ensure that a representative number of members from protected classes are applying for jobs. If, for example, one finds that few African-Americans are applying for jobs at your library despite that fact that 20 percent of the local area workforce is African-American, then the library should be concerned.

2. By using an applicant flow log for specific positions. An applicant flow log is used to track the disposition of applications as they progress through the hiring process. Such a log might consist of the name of all applicants, and spaces to indicate whether the applicant was interviewed, and whether the applicant was selected. Spaces should also be provided to explain for each applicant the reason for rejecting or selecting the applicant.

3. By summarizing and analyzing data regarding all hiring decisions made at the end of the fiscal or calendar year. Through examination of the rate at which members of protected classes are being hired, the employer may find that discriminatory practices, albeit unintentional, may be occurring (see discussion in Chapter 2).

4 RECRUITING EFFECTIVE EMPLOYEES

GENERAL FACTORS AFFECTING RECRUITMENT

Public employers are under increasing pressure to increase the productivity of their workers. Many members of the public have become impatient and skeptical regarding the motivation and energy exerted by those who work and supervise in the public sector. Whether the reputation of public employees is deserved is not as important as the fact that employers have come under increased scrutiny concerning the output of their workforce. For this reason alone, organizations need to recruit effectively. Effective recruitment has the advantage of maintaining a qualified pool of applicants to fill vacant positions as they arise.

All employers are looking for the same thing: effective employees. The search for the effective employee is a complex process which must take into account a wide variety of factors. One must keep in mind that a library's workforce is heterogeneous. Many different types of workers must be recruited depending on the classification of jobs needed. These classifications include library directors and administrators, department and branch heads, degreed librarians, library assistants, clerical and secretarial workers, maintenance workers, graphic artists, security personnel, shelvers, and volunteers. More than two-thirds of library employees are in support classifications. Different recruiting strategies may be needed depending on the job.

In general, recruitment is affected by the following factors:

Laborforce trends: Library organizations are affected by trends in the laborforce locally and nationally. These trends can be related to the workforce in general or in the library profession in particular.

General economic conditions: Under poor economic conditions, business and social agencies may be cutting back. This may make recruiting much easier if the library budget is not as seriously affected. In contrast, healthy business climates can create a shortage of available workers which drives wages up. In addition, the economic status of the community will have a bearing on recruitment. Communities in which have a large number of two family income earners, or single parent families usually provide a rich source for library workers.

Competing businesses or agencies: In areas with high demand for clerical, public service or information workers it is much more difficult to recruit and retain workers for the library. In areas where there is a glut of such skilled workers, recruitment will be much easier.

Perception of the Geographic area and community: Potential employees are much more likely to relocate or remain in areas which are perceived to have pleasant surroundings. Of course, the factors that are perceived as desirable will vary from person to person. Obviously such factors as climate, proximity to cultural or recreational facilities, cost of living, schools, and housing are important for many prospective employees. Other factors may include proximity to large cities or country-side, shopping, ethnic similarities, and proximity to family.

Available skills of the workforce: Recruitment is much easier where the skills and education levels meet the demands of the library. In locations where reading levels, technical, and professional education are low, recruitment may prove much more challenging. The challenge for librarianship is considerable especially because libraries will need both traditionally literate and also computer literate populations from which to draw its workforce. This problem may become especially acute among support staff workers because of the potential mismatch between the skills required by libraries and the lack of general and computer skills in the work population. Nor can libraries depend on an oversupply of college graduates which, according to the Bureau of National Affairs, is shrinking.[1]

Wage competitiveness: Employees are bound to compare what they can earn in your organization to other positions in your area or in the case of managers and professionals even outside of your area. A competitive salary is more likely to be part of an effective recruiting strategy. This may be an especially difficult problem for libraries. If growth in jobs will increase greater than the growth in the labor force, then the price of labor (wages) is bound to rise. If funding growth is slow or non-existent, libraries will find themselves at an increasing disadvantage.

Proximity of library education programs: The presence or absence of library education programs can have a profound effect on the availability of degreed professionals. In areas where library schools are distant, the cost and difficulty of recruitment will be substantially greater and may lead libraries to substitute support staff or individuals with other types of degrees for individuals with library degrees.

Reputation of the organization: Many employees are aware at the time of application of the reputation of the library. Libraries with reputations for excellence as well as good pay and benefits are more likely to attract excellent candidates. Of course, other factors also affect the decision to apply for a position, but reputation can improve recruitment especially when there is strong competition for workers.

Perception of the organization's and job's ability to meet employee needs and expectations: Recruitment is a two-way process and must be viewed from two perspectives: that of the organization and that of the prospective employee. Recruitment not only involves finding employees who can satisfy the needs of the organization; it also involves selecting individuals whose needs will be satisfied by the organization. It is not productive to select employees who are hard-working, but who will not be satisfied to work in the organization; such individuals will simply leave when the time is right. This suggests strongly that the employer delve into more than just job knowledge and skills, but also work values and attitudes. The library employer must look for a "fit" between the worker and the library. This fit is not only to the organizational culture as a whole, but to the particular work tasks, supervisory climate, and working conditions. The employer asks questions such as: "Can the employee do the job? Will he or she be able to work with others? Will he or she be cooperative employee? What is the potential for promotion?" In contrast, employees will ask themselves other important questions:

> Does the job provide enough money?
> Does the job provide enough status?
> Are certain jobs of higher status?
> Are the working conditions good?
> Are there better opportunities in this area?
> Are there better opportunities elsewhere?
> Am I locked in to this area?

Do I really want to do this kind of work?

Does the job provide an opportunity for growth?

This last question is especially interesting in librarianship. Heim has noted that certain positions such as technical services and children's work are perceived as having little potential for growth. This makes recruitment for these positions especially difficult.[2]

CURRENT WORKFORCE FACTORS

One of the most important aspects of recruitment is the trends in the general workforce. An overview of workforce trends is instructive in attempting to assess future recruitment efforts of library employers. In terms of the general workforce, at least four trends are relevant:

Job growth in general will be greater than labor market growth: As a rule this means that fewer workers will be competing for more jobs. Employers will be forced to provide incentives to attract and retain employees. Recruitment efforts will have to increase and become more sophisticated.

The general workforce is aging: The median age of workers is expected to be 39 by the year 2000. More and more applicants should be expected to come from older workers. Employers must consider what recruitment strategies are most effective with these age groups, especially in terms of salary, benefits, professional development, and working conditions. The Bureau of National Affairs notes that recruitment strategies should concentrate on the needs of individuals between 25-54 who will comprise the major share of the workforce. The cohorts of younger and older workers will become smaller in the near term. If the pool of potential applicants is geographically distant, it must also be remembered that mobility decreases with age.[3]

The major laborforce growth will come from minorities, women, and immigrants: While 55% of the laborforce was composed of white males in 1972, by the year 2000, only 45%

of the workforce will be so composed.[4] Eighty percent of the laborforce growth to the year 2000 will come from minority youth, women, and immigrants.[5] Employers will need to become more sensitive to the needs of these groups not only in terms of recruitment incentives but also in terms of working conditions. It is senseless to hire a minority employee only to create dissatisfaction through an unresponsive workplace. This is demoralizing to the employee, increases the liability of the employer, and is uneconomic overall. The focus of the increasing proportion of minorities is expected to be concentrated in support classifications rather than on the professional levels. The major reason for this is that although minorities are a rapidly growing part of the workforce, they are more likely to be deprived of higher education. They will represent, therefore, a disproportionately greater part of the under-educated workforce. This trend is confirmed in librarianship in that the minority representation in library schools is actually declining.[6]

Technological change in the workplace will continue at a rapid pace: The nature of job tasks, especially those in the information professions will evolve continuously as will the skills required to perform them and the work environment in which they are performed. Employers will need to identify and retain workers who are very adaptable, motivated by a challenge, and able to master and apply new information quickly. It may also mean that certain support staff skills (e.g., desktop publishing and file management) may be increasingly valued skills which require new recruitment incentives and methods of recognizing the status and importance of such individuals.

In addition to these general trends, there are also some trends within the library profession that are worth noting:

There are a substantial number of librarians who are approaching retirement age: As of 1986, more than one in five librarians was over the age of 55.[7] This would suggest that there should be considerable opportunity for hiring in the next ten years. This is counterbalanced by at least two other forces that are mentioned below.

The employee turnover rate of librarians is very low: The annual turnover rate of librarians averages about 7 percent.[8] This means that employers have relatively few opportunities to hire librarians. This does not mean, however, that the hiring process is unimportant. Quite the opposite. Because of the stability of the professional workforce, each opportunity to replace a worker must be valued as a rare chance to maintain or improve the employer's workforce.

Projections for state and local government to the year 2010 indicate that fiscal growth will be very slow: This trend has substantial effect on recruitment efforts. First, the available money to recruit and hire library staff will be hard to come by. Travelling funds for recruitment or expense money to bring in candidates may be severely curtailed. Second, it may change the focus of recruitment strategies in that it may provide an incentive for library boards to substitute support staff for degreed librarians. Although from a perspective of quality library service this may be problematic, decreasing funds may even increase support/professional staff ratios in the years to come.

The number of library school graduates is decreasing: As the number of library schools decline, the number of graduates have concomitantly been reduced. This places a strain on the recruitment efforts of libraries. Libraries will have to be more ingenious and perhaps need to offer more incentives to attract appropriate workers. Heim has noted that recruitment strategies of some employers are becoming more aggressive—good candidates are offered positions before they come out of library school. Candidates then can target courses that are more appropriate for the type of library in which they will work.[9] Of course, the reduction in the number of library school graduates may also have the effect of stimulating the hiring of support staff for positions normally requiring the degreed librarian if serious shortages arise.

The number of library schools is decreasing: Over the last decade there has been a substantial decrease in the number of accredited library schools. Regardless of the effect on the number of library school graduates, it places an especially difficult burden on the recruitment efforts of library organizations that are subsequently forced to draw their degreed librarians from much greater distances. It is difficult to get individuals to come long distances for interviews, especially if the organization has limited financial resources to compensate for expenses. Also, given the relatively low salaries of librarians, this problem becomes doubly difficult because the prospective employee must calculate the expense, sacrifice, and gamble taken to relocate long distances to an unfamiliar geographic area.

It is difficult to predict what the net effect of these countervailing forces will have on the hiring process. At the least, library employers should expect that the recruitment process will be more expensive and challenging. More minorities will be applying for entry level positions especially in support staff jobs and support staff categories will become a major focus for recruitment incentives. There will probably be little extra money for acquiring additional staff but replacement staff will become necessary in order to fill positions vacated by retiring workers. In addition, new hires may be older and possess new skills that will have to be recognized by the employers. All this means that new recruitment and retention strategies will be needed to attract and retain effective library workers.

RECRUITMENT STRATEGIES

Recruitment strategies are not merely objective measures taken by an organization to locate good workers. Such strategies reflect a particular philosophy toward the library profession and the philosophy of service to be provided by the specific library. Library employers that simply look for the cheapest worker are saying something different than employers who spend time and effort recruiting the best qualified people. There are hidden dangers in recruitment strategies that acquire the lowest cost worker or that ignore the need for professional knowledge and experience. Aside from endangering the profession, it reinforces low expectations on the part of the public. Unless the public perceives library work as a professional skill, it is less likely to support it when financial constraints force tough decisions on the part of public officials.

Effective recruitment requires that the employer be knowledgeable about a variety of factors including how to locate the best sources for candidates, what are the prevailing and competitive wages for the position being recruited, and what wage philosophy regarding pay rate will be offered in relation to the prevailing wages. The employer must also be aware of average lead time needed for applicants for various positions, and the true costs of recruitment efforts, especially in regard to the recruitment plan.

For example, if the employer can afford it, offering to pay all or part of the relocation costs might tip the balance in favor of acquiring a new employee.

Effective recruitment also requires that the employer create a work environment that is as attractive as possible to a potential candidate. This means good wage and benefit packages, and special attention to policies responsive to women such as flexible scheduling, compressed work weeks, part-year employment, job sharing, and telecommuting, as well as family leaves.

In preparation for recruitment, organizations should have at least one individual responsible for developing recruitment strategies and for implementing them. In recognition of the importance of recruitment in business, the Bureau of National Affairs has noted that human resource departments are evolving into strategic planning and marketing functions rather than as service providers.[10] As libraries compete in a tighter job market, their individuals responsible for recruitment will also have to become marketing specialists.

INTERNAL RECRUITMENT SOURCES

Employee referral programs: Current staff may be excellent sources for potential employees. These individuals have personal knowledge of the candidate and they have a stake in the performance of the new employee. Poor performance would reflect badly on the employee who referred him or her. In order to encourage staff to provide the names of potential candidates, the employer might conduct workshops or meetings telling staff the importance of locating good potential employees for the organization. Some employers have begun incentive programs. These programs offer such blandishments as monetary awards or gifts if the referred employee turns out to be a successful worker. Overall, this recruiting technique is inexpensive. However, there are some disadvantages to the process of employee referral. One problem is that the employer may feel an obligation to hire the referred employee or risk bad feeling with the current staff member. Similarly, the employer may feel uncomfortable in implementing disciplinary action against the new employee and fear that the referring employee may also become disruptive in retaliation.[11] Finally, one must be very careful about "word-of-mouth" recruitment techniques. In organizations in which a disproportionately low number of minorities or other protected classes are present, such recruitment techniques tend to perpetuate the current workforce composition. When used alone, this might well be considered a discriminatory practice and substantially increase the employer's liability for a discrimination suit. Some of these problems are eliminated when one uses *former* employees as a source of referral. In so far as the former employee was a good performer and is aware of the current needs of the library, such referrals may prove quite useful.

Internal promotion programs: Some libraries have a policy of promoting from within. Although having a hard and fast policy is not recommended, libraries should consider having career ladders for staff. Such ladders should make clear what additional knowledge and skill is required to move to the next position. Staff should then be given the opportunity to acquire this knowledge and skill. Internal promotion has the distinct advantage that the individual's performance and work attitudes have already been observed. This makes prediction of job success much easier. It has the disadvantage of tending to exclude new blood which is sometimes important in reinvigorating an organization.

Application files: Most libraries should have a system by which individuals can apply for positions by filling out applications, even when no particular job vacancy exists. A major advantage of such files is that they provide a ready pool of applicants that can be consulted as the need arises. If the applicant form is properly designed, one can readily determine which applications are appropriate for the specific position. A drawback to such files is that many applications become out of date rapidly as the applicants accept other positions or relocate. For this reason, applicant files should remain active for relatively short periods of time (three to six months). These files should be weeded in a timely fashion so that time is not spent going through out-of-date applications.

In addition, the quality of the application files will increase if the employer has liberal, clearly stated hours for application. In this way, strong potential applicants will not be turned away. Similarly, the quality of the application could be improved if screening interviews are conducted at the same time that an application is submitted. The purpose of a screening interview is to get a basic idea of the candidate's job interests, work experience, and educational background. Sometimes an employer can determine a great deal about an applicant's general suitability for library work through these interviews. Since most applicants who fill out applications as walk-ins would not be aware of the screening interview before coming in, the employer should have alternative hours at which time the applicant can return for the screening interview.

Recruiting for professional positions: When recruiting librarians from the library's current support staff workforce, it is important to understand that career choice is a developmental process. Individuals do not simply decide one day what career they wish to pursue, rather career choices are slowly narrowed down based on a variety of personal and job experiences. Job choice is affected not only by one's personal background and experience as children and young adults, it is also shaped by past experiences in jobs, current job experiences, and expectations of future positions. Currently employed support staff members will evaluate the benefits of continued and improved employment opportunities within the library profession against occupational possibilities outside the library. Current experiences are especially important in the library in helping the support staff employee evaluate whether librarianship can meet the employee's future job expectations. It is a wise investment to create opportunities for good support staff to see the challenges and benefits of library work. It is also important to recognize that the library should encourage and develop only those employees who have potential to be good librarians. Among the techniques that might be employed are the following:

- Providing career ladders for support staff so that they receive progressively more challenging work associated with the duties of professional librarians.
- Providing financial assistance for professional education through grants and scholarships. Such grants should provide a guarantee of employment on the professional level after completion of the degree.
- Asking library educators to meet with selected support staff interested in librarianship as a career.
- Providing opportunities for professional development in workshops and programs both inside and outside the library.

- Providing support for employees to attend state and national conferences where exposure to professional ideas would be increased.

EXTERNAL RECRUITING SOURCES

Obtaining names of potential applicants: When higher level positions, such as directorships, are being recruited, it is sometimes useful to contact individuals by phone or mail who might be interested in the position or who might know others who would be interested. These referrals could then be sent letters indicating that their names had been submitted as a prospective candidate. It is useful to include a job description in the letter, as well as the job advertisement if one is available.

Sending letters to possible candidates: As noted above, when higher level positions are being recruited, the employer should consider sending letters to individuals whom the employer believes would make good candidates for the position. These letters indicate the type of position open and may include a sample job description.

"Point of purchase" recruiting: In this type of recruiting, the application form is placed in an area where patrons are most likely to be using library services. For example, one may find application forms in fast food establishments at the food-service counter. In libraries, the most likely place would be the circulation desk or reference desk. Application forms could be placed at these points to encourage potential candidates.

Employment databases and telephone hotlines: A variety of states now make job openings available through telephone hotlines. Because this is a relatively novel source of job openings, employers may well be tapping an entirely different group of potential employees by listing their vacancies in these sources. Lists of joblines for librarians are printed intermittently in *American Libraries.*

Local High Schools and Colleges: In many cases, schools and colleges sponsor recruiting events for prospective employers. These might be open houses or job fairs. At such places, the employer may be able to set up a booth and talk to interested students. Similarly, open houses provide the employer an opportunity to meet prospective students and possibly examine the training program's facilities. Job fairs and open houses can be good sources especially for shelvers and other support positions. It may also be an opportunity to encourage students to pursue professional education in librarianship. Other opportunities to make contacts in high schools involve making presentations to counselors or to students in their classrooms. Schools usually have bulletin boards on which job vacancies can be posted. Colleges and universities also have placement offices where jobs can be posted. Interview rooms are often provided in these facilities and student reference files are also maintained for the employer's inspection.

Consultants and Search Firms: For upper-level positions, the employer may wish to retain a consultant or search firm. The consultant or firm may be involved in any number of steps in the hiring process. Their participation could involve conducting hiring, training, identifying prospective candidates, screening resumes and applications, interviewing candidates, checking references, reducing the number of candidates to a small number and ranking them, and/or being part of the final selection process. The degree of participation is up to the employer. Of course, the greater the degree of participation, the greater the expense. Consultants or search firms can be very useful in the hiring process. They provide an objective perspective on candidates, may know novel sources for recruitment, and are usually experienced at the hiring process. Drawbacks include expense and a lack of knowledge about actual library processes. The use of consultants or firms is not a panacea for effective hiring; the employer must still have a very clear idea of the job to be filled and the desired characteristics of the individual who must fill it. This information must be communicated precisely to the consultant.

Employment bureaus and agencies: Maintaining regular contact with agencies or organizations that can locate potential applicants is an important part of the recruitment process. This is especially true for support staff positions. Among the agencies that can prove useful are the state Bureau of Employment Services, the local NAACP or Urban League, and the American Association of Retired Persons. One must be very careful that the referring agency understand the nature of the library work to be performed. Individuals in referral agencies may seriously underestimate the knowledge and skills needed to perform support services. When inappropriate individuals are referred, this wastes the time and money of the organization and the individual who has taken the time to apply.

Training and vocational schools: The need for employees with strong clerical backgrounds is still great. Many vocational and technical schools provide the training necessary to perform these functions. Like public schools, colleges, and universities, these institutions often offer open houses and job fairs for prospective employers.

Other libraries or organizations associated with libraries: Many libraries as well as library networks or consortia are willing, on a reciprocating basis, to post job notices from requesting libraries. This is a good source of recruitment in that the prospective candidates are bound to possess at least some library experience and are familiar with the library environment.

Other service organizations: A generally untapped source of candidates is from organizations whose employees may have similar service values to those of the library. In this case, school systems which post job notices for teachers or employers of social service workers may identify individuals who wish to continue service to the community but in a different capacity.

Professional Associations and Conferences: National associations such as the American Library Association (ALA) and the American Society of Information Scientists provide job placement centers for employers who can inspect resumes and interview candidates for job openings.

THE RECRUITMENT INTERVIEW

In the recruiting process, it is useful for the library to add to its applicant pool by conducting interviews even when no position is open. Sources where interviews can be conducted include library conferences, such as at the annual ALA conference which offers a placement bureau for this purpose; other sources are library schools, job fairs, or vocational and technical schools. The recruitment interview differs from the selection interview in several ways. First, it is usually spontaneous; there may be a little advance warning, but as a rule, there is little preparation time for either the interviewee or the interviewer. Second, the purpose of the recruitment interview is as much to interest a prospective candidate in the library as it is to assess the specific credentials of the potential applicant. Because information-giving is critical in this sense, the recruiter should have good written information materials available and be able to sell the organization. This also highlights the importance of having effective recruiters. They must be able to convey enthusiasm, to emphasize the meaningfulness and potential of the work, and to promote applications from individuals deemed appropriate for employment.

ADVERTISING FOR POSITIONS

An obvious tool for recruitment when a position is open is the use of job advertisements. It is important for the employer to assess precisely which advertising strategy would target the right type of worker. The job advertisement has five basic purposes:[12]

> To attract suitable candidates.
>
> To motivate appropriate readers to reply.
>
> To eliminate those readers who are not appropriate.
>
> To reach appropriate candidates as economically as possible.
>
> To enhance the overall reputation of the library by the image projected by the advertisement.

Generally, the job advertisement provides several categories of information divided into five sections. The order and detail of each section may vary, but the general order is as follows:

Title and location of the position: This should be of a characteristic type size and font to be noticed.

Brief description of the job: This section should describe the type of library, philosophy of service, and basic job responsibilities. It should include motivating comments on the opportunity and challenge of the position as well as any other notable non-monetary benefits. This might even include a statement about the geographic area and climate.

The required knowledge, skills, and abilities of the job: This should include degrees and experience required or preferred and special skills and aptitudes needed.

Compensation: The salary or salary range should be included as well as a review of available benefits. Remember that benefits not only include insurance, but such perks as retirement, paid vacation, sick time and other leaves, and paid conference travel.

Closing information: Information on the type of materials that should be sent, including such items as cover letters, resumes, job references, or names of referees. The advertisement should also include a closing date for application and the name and address of the individual to whom the materials should be sent. Whenever appropriate, the end of the advertisement should include a statement that the employer is committed to Affirmative Action/Equal Opportunity Employment.

SOURCES FOR ADVERTISING

Selecting the right place for advertising is essential given the expense of advertising in most publications. Costs of advertising will vary drastically depending on the publication. Investigation should be done concerning advertising rates before making a commitment.

Advertising strategy depends in large part on the geographic area to be targeted and the type of individual the employer wants to attract. Strategies will differ if one is looking for a director, a librarian, or a support staff worker. In all cases, the library should make its advertisement sufficiently attractive to draw the attention of the reader. When considering in which source to advertise, the employer should consider how many times the advertisement will appear and when it will appear. In addition, whenever possible, the library should try to secure an especially good location in the publication where the advertisement will be placed, but this is not often under the control of the employer, or may require a prohibitive cost.

Newspapers: A common source of advertising for support staff positions is the newspaper. There are many types of newspapers including the major daily newspaper, a neighborhood weekly, public school and college newspapers, club or organization newspapers, and newspapers that target special populations such as those distributed primarily to specific ethnic groups. Neighborhood newspapers might be especially useful for branch library vacancies; ethnic newspapers in situations where the library is attempting to recruit minorities; and public school newspapers if the library is looking for shelvers.

Newspapers can also be used in attempting to locate librarians and administrative positions. In cases where the library wishes to recruit from a national perspective, advertisements might be placed in major urban newspapers such as the *New York Times* or *Los Angeles Times*.

Journals: A more frequent source for advertising for librarian or administrative positions are professional journals. The library profession has several prominent sources including *Library Journal, American Libraries, Library Journal Hotline,* among others. In cases where computer or information science expertise is required, the *Journal of the American Society of Information Science* may be more appropriate.

Posters and notices: A job advertisement might also be prepared on a poster or on a single-sheet notice. Such items can be placed in high-traffic areas where members of the public pass. Generally this technique would be used for support staff positions. Posters or notices could be placed on school, college, and community bulletin boards as well as on public transportation.

Brochures: For high-level positions, such as directors, the institution may find that it is worth the expense to create a brochure. The brochure might contain general information about the library system and its philosophy of service, the community served, the duties of the position and the qualifications sought, the benefits of the job, and the application process. Notable aspects of the geographic area might also be included. The brochure should be designed with aesthetics as well as information value in mind and contain photographs of the institution and the area.

Videos: Videos can be an effective way to give a prospective applicant a closer look at the library. As a rule the video should have a generic quality so that it can be used in the recruitment of a variety of positions. Videos expose the applicant to the actual look and sounds of the workplace. They are able to provide a more personal glimpse of working conditions, the current staff, and patrons in the normal work setting. The values of the institution can also be conveyed especially in terms of public service through comments and examples of patron-staff interactions. Specific staff members such as the library director and other key personnel can be introduced. Generally, such videos run no more than 15 minutes and, as a rule, they should be produced professionally. They can be used in many settings: at booths at library conferences, at job fairs, or in the home of a candidate. Although initial costs may be substantial, copies can be made at low cost and are well worth the money if it helps to recruit effective workers.

REDUCING THE NEED TO RECRUIT

Because of the substantial cost of recruiting and hiring staff, the best alternative is to create a workforce of satisfied and productive workers who are inclined to remain with organization. In order to accomplish this, it is the responsibility of the employer to create a workplace in which job commitment and productivity are part of the "corporate culture." This includes using the following organizational techniques:

Provide opportunities for interesting and challenging work: Most staff want their work situation to provide some satisfaction. Generally, routine and repetitive tasks are associated with lower levels of satisfaction. Consequently, the employer should make every effort to provide job variety.

Emphasize the meaningfulness of work: Job commitment is associated with the extent to which employees feel that they are accomplishing something important. This should be relatively easy in the library setting because the functions that they perform are readily accepted as important to the community and the individual. For example, the importance of the library to young people and to the elderly can be easily conveyed and demonstrated. The employer should take whatever opportunities are available to emphasize that the work of each library staff member is critical to the overall success of these altruistic goals.

Emphasize the interdependence of the work: Job commitment is also related to the employee's recognition that other employees and departments depend on what she does. An individual who believes that no one else relies on her will feel free to leave; employees who feel interconnected will feel a responsibility to remain. This sense of interdependence can also be increased by permitting participatory decision making on the departmental level, and for the setting of group (departmental) performance goals as well as individual goals.

Emphasize the opportunities to make social bonds: Individuals who feel alienated or unconnected to the organization are much more likely to leave it. The organization should provide numerous opportunities for friendships and professional bonds to form. This can occur through assignment to committees, staff meetings, social get-togethers, and work assignments that emphasize interpersonal communications and cooperative action.

Provide recognition: Employees want to feel appreciated for the work they perform. For this reason, the employer should recognize employee performance both financially and psychologically. Most library employees do not expect to receive substantial increases in pay, but they do expect to get some increase. In addition, supervisors should be trained to compliment employees and work groups regularly when employees perform well, and to provide opportunities for staff recognition at larger gatherings for excellence in performance.

Provide good staff development and training: Many employees want to grow in their jobs in order to feel that they have potential and talents that would permit them greater responsibilities and to move up within the organization. Libraries, like many other organizations, provide relatively few resources for training and development. Training and developing staff not only improves productivity, but it permits the organization to fill vacancies with internal applicants as job opportunities arise. This is, in the end, less expensive than having to recruit from the outside.

Provide human resource policies that are flexible and respond to the needs of the library workforce: Library policies and practices are not only intended to maintain order, they send a message to the employee. If that message is that the employee is respected and that the employer cares about the employee, then there is a much greater chance that employee turnover will be low. This message can be sent through strong health insurance programs, accommodations for disabilities and transportation benefits, fiscal resources for conference travel and workshops, and benefits that reflect the predominantly female character of the workforce such as day care, flexible work scheduling, and job sharing.

Develop a hiring system that identifies the right individual for the job: It is essential that recruitment efforts be well planned and directed toward specific groups of potential employees with the required knowledge, skills, and abilities. In addition, the hiring system must use appropriate techniques and be thorough in investigating the abilities and attitudes of job candidates so the appropriate selection can be made. Good hiring means less need to hire again.

ISSUES IN MINORITY RECRUITMENT

The recruitment of minorities has been a sensitive and important issue for the library profession over the years. Wright has noted that efforts to recruit minorities have been prompted in at least three ways: Federal Affirmative Action Guidelines and assistance programs for undergraduates, graduates, and professional education; caucuses advocating the underrepresented in professional organizations; and the use of moral persuasion.[13]

Clearly, many in the library profession still feel that these efforts, although noble and earnest, have not created a professional workforce that accurately reflects the needs of minorities and other protected classes. The evidence is discouraging. The number of minorities receiving degrees appears to be declining. In 1979, minorities represented nearly 10 percent of all master's degree graduates; by 1984 this dropped to just above 6 percent.[14]

The commitment to the recruitment of minorities is essential if libraries are to overcome the unfortunate perception by many that they are institutions designed to serve the white middle and upper classes. The hiring of minorities does not, in and of itself, dissolve the inhospitalities that many minorities perceive, but it can make a substantial contribution toward increasing the sensitivity of the organization to their needs.

In this context, it should be said again that career choice is not usually a one-time event. It is a process in which choices are influenced by current and past experiences. For this reason, recruitment of minority professionals may be direct as when interviewing takes place in library schools, or it may be indirect in which a minority staff member is recruited into a support position and then a concerted effort is made to provide positive experiences in the workplace, so that the employee will subsequently select librarianship as a career.

There is considerable evidence that most employee turnover occurs within the first few years of library service. Successful recruitment of minorities implies that the employee remain with the organization. In order to help integrate the employee into the organization, the employer should consider the use of internships or mentorships. In either of these cases, the new employee is guided by a more senior and respected member of the organization. The intern supervisor or mentor can orient the employee, make the employee feel comfortable, answer questions or concerns, serve as an advocate for the employee, give general advice and counsel on how to succeed with the organization, and serve as a constructive role model.

It is essential that libraries develop aggressive recruitment programs rather than being passive and waiting for minority candidates to make application. Aggressive strategies are to the advantage of the library, because it places much greater control in the hands of the employer. With aggressive strategies, the library can identify and evaluate possible candidates and encourage those who have considerable potential to apply. If the library is passive, control is lost. Below are a few suggestions for aggressive recruitment:

- Go on recruitment trips to library schools where a substantial proportion of the student body consists of minorities.

- Develop networks with prominent members of your minority communities, who can serve as communication conduits to individuals and organizations.

- Use current and former minority members of your staff as sources of information and provide rewards (especially for current employees) if the referred candidate becomes a successful employee.

- Develop a promotion program that identifies agencies in the community that serve minorities and could provide names of potential applicants.

- Advertise all relevant positions with community agencies that provide services to minorities such as the Urban Leagues, the NAACP, ethnic newspapers, and other similar community services.

- Provide orientation programs to minority community leaders and guidance counselors regarding the benefits and nature of library service.

- Develop scholarship programs that would provide substantial financial assistance for minorities to attend a library school. Employers should consider local charities, foundations, civic organizations, or philanthropists who could endow a fund for the purpose of minority recruitment.

- Send notices of job vacancies for posting to employers with similar public service values which may employ many minorities (e.g., social service agencies, school systems which have a substantial minority enrollment).

- Provide minority support staff with ample opportunity for challenging work, training and development which promotes the desire to become a degreed librarian.

- Attend programs and consult materials sponsored by the ALA Black Caucus and other library associations or association units dealing with the concerns of minorities.

REFERENCES

1. Fernandez, Linda. *Now Hiring: An Employer's Guide to Recruiting in a Tight Labor Market.* Washington, D.C.: Bureau of National Affairs, 1989, p. 27.

2. Heim, Kathleen M. "Organizational Entry: Human Resources Selection and Adaptation in Response to a Complex Labor Pool," *Library Trends* 38 (Summer 1989): p. 24.

3. Fernandez, p. A12-14.

4. Fernandez, p. 3.

5. Fernandez, p. A11.

6. Abdullahi, Ismail. "Recruitment and Mentoring of Minority Students," *Journal of Education for Library and Information Science* 33 (Fall 1992): 308.

7. Rubin, Richard. *Human Resources Management in Libraries: Theory and Practice.* New York: Neal-Schuman, 1992, p. 6.

8. Neal, James, "Employee Turnover and the Exit Interview." Presentation given at the Allerton Institute, November 7, 1987, University of Illinois at Urbana-Champaign; and Richard Rubin, "Employee Turnover Among Full-Time Public Librarians," *Library Quarterly* 59 (January 1989): 37-38.

9. Heim, p. 29.

10. Fernandez, p. 5.

11. Jackson, Mathew. *Recruiting, Interviewing, and Selecting: A Manual for Line Managers.* London: McGraw-Hill, 1972, p. 28; and Fernandez, p. C-11.

12. Jackson, p. 30.

13. Wright, Joyce C. "Recruitment and Retention of Minorities in Academic Libraries: A Plan of Action for the 1990s," *Illinois Libraries* 72 (November 1990): 621.

14. Brown, Lorene E., "A Crisis in Librarianship: The Decline in the Number of Minorities Entering the Profession Since 1979." Presentation at the Midwinter Meeting of the ALA Black Caucus as cited in Joyce C. Wright, "Recruitment and Retention of Minorities in Academic Libraries: A Plan of Action for the 1990s," *Illinois Libraries* 72 (November 1990): 621.

5 CONDUCTING A HIRING PROCESS

STEP 1: GETTING A FULL UNDER-STANDING OF THE SPECIFIC JOB

Once the organization has the necessary prerequisites for effective hiring, it is ready to begin hiring. For each opening, it is extremely important to understand precisely what the job is. At first glance, the issue seems easy: the job is defined as the tasks which the employee is supposed to accomplish. Certainly, the specific tasks of the job are very important and those involved in the selection process should draw on current job descriptions as well as discussions with relevant staff in determining the precise duties required. But job tasks are only one part of it. Jobs must be understood in a much broader context. A job is not only a set of defined tasks, it has a context, a relationship with other positions and individuals within the organization as a whole. Each job or set of jobs has a definite character or nature that distinguishes it from other jobs. Each position carries with it particular responsibilities and demands.

The employer must search for employees who can perform in this broader sense. For this reason, before one considers hiring for a particular position, the employer must understand well the character of that position and develop hiring criteria and interview questions that predict if a candidate is suited to this character.

One method of understanding the context of a particular job is to use the tools of job analysis. These tools are normally applied when an organization is developing job descriptions, job classifications, and wage and salary ranges for an organization as a whole. But it can also be used effectively to develop a richer picture of a particular position. A common method of analyzing a job is to examine it in terms of various job factors. Among these factors are the following:

Job knowledge: This includes all the skills and knowledge needed to perform the job at an acceptable level. Some jobs require only that the individual have the skills and ability to follow basic instructions and perform simple work routines; other jobs may require special knowledge such as use of computers, while others may require knowledge of professional principles and practices. One needs to know clearly exactly what skills and levels of knowledge are needed to perform the job well.

Problem-solving ability: This involves the amount of analysis, evaluation, creativity, and reasoning required in order to make sound decisions on the job. Some jobs require very little decision making because the routines performed are circumscribed by clear rules and well-defined routines. In contrast, some positions are guided by basic policies and principles, but not by specific rules or instructions, and in some cases, some jobs merely have general policies or organizational goals that guide the regular decision-making of the position. If a position is guided by clear rules and routines, the employer should not necessarily require the skills and abilities of a creative decision maker. In contrast, if the position requires considerable creativity and analytical abilities, one needs to formulate strategies to try to evaluate those characteristics.

Freedom of action: This factor considers the availability, frequency, and nature of supervision after the employee has received the necessary basic training. In some positions, the supervisor may closely supervise and direct the activities of the employee and review work often and carefully. In other positions, an employee may receive only very general supervision and work is reviewed infrequently. Other positions may have little or no direct supervision and the employee has considerable freedom in the job. Employers need to consider exactly how much freedom there is in a position and select individuals who are comfortable with the type of supervisory environment and control that is exercised in the particular job.

Contact with others: This factor considers the level of responsibility that the employee bears for meeting or influencing others. It includes contact with employees and with the public. Some positions require no contact with the public and very little with staff; others involve daily contact. Still others have infrequent contacts with the public, but what contacts there are may be very important, affecting the survival and well-being of the library. Understanding the number, type, and importance of these contacts should shape the type of information that should be obtained from candidates for a particular job. Similarly, when it comes to staff contacts, the employer should understand clearly what types of regular, formal, and informal contacts are essential in the performance of the job, including those that fall outside the immediate work area of the employee.

Complexity: This factor deals with the variety and difficulty of the tasks of the job. Jobs vary considerably regarding the judgement, initiative, and creativity required to perform them. Some jobs have a limited number of activities and the tasks are well defined, requiring little individual judgement or ingenuity; other jobs may require a considerable amount of independent judgement in vital management areas such as supervision and coordination of activities. Still other positions may include not only considerable judgment and initiative but may be involved in the creation of policies and practices for the organization as a whole. Individuals should be selected that match their ability to deal with the complexity of the tasks of the job.

Supervision: This factor deals with the amount and type of supervision that is required. The term *supervision* is ambiguous and should be defined clearly for each position. For example, supervision can mean scheduling for some employers; in other libraries supervision may entail much more such as responsibility for hiring, training and developing, evaluating, disciplining, and terminating staff. In order to understand the job in terms of supervision, the employer must consider the number of employees, the type of employee supervised (e.g., professional, support, part-time, full-time), the variety of employees, and the actual activities that make up supervision. Only then can appropriate criteria and questioning strategies be developed.

Accountability/responsibility (impact of error): This factor involves the amount of opportunity for error in the job and the seriousness of the consequences of the error. Some positions have clearly defined duties where error is less likely and the impact of the error may be small and confined to the specific work area. Other positions in which highly complex tasks are performed may have a much higher possibility of error and the impact may affect many departments or the entire organization. For positions in which an error could be critical, such as a director's position, it may be vital to explore the individual's judgment, ingenuity, and decision-making abilities.

Confidentiality: This factor involves whether the position requires creating, organizing, communicating, and controlling access to confidential information or records. Some positions deal with few records or pieces of information that are not public, while other positions may deal with personnel and financial records, highly sensitive administrative and legal correspondence and reports, or collective bargaining material. If confidentiality is an important issue in a position, the knowledge and skills of prospective candidates in understanding the responsibilities of confidentiality should be carefully explored.

Working conditions: Working conditions deal with those aspects of the work environment that may produce stress and affect the health and safety of employees. Some positions are situated in well-regulated environments with few environmental dangers or threats from the public; in other jobs, employees may be exposed to extreme heat or cold, noxious fumes or dangerous equipment, or belligerent members of the public. It is important to determine whether a potential employee is willing to work effectively under the real working conditions of the job.

It is critical that the employer considers what the job really is, not what the employer would like the job to be. Only then can realistic job issues be explored. Whenever a job opening occurs, those engaged in the selection process should review the basic job factors that describe the character of the job. If the organization has already gone through a formal job analysis, there may be existing current information for review. Some of this information may be provided in the job description. If such information is not available, the selectors should ask themselves questions that relate to factors similar to the ones identified above. Focus should be on the current job as it is to be performed, not necessarily how it was performed in the past. Below are a list of questions that may contribute to a broader understanding of a particular job:

1. What is the main purpose of the job?
2. What are the most frequently performed tasks in the job?
3. What are the most important functions of the job?
4. To what extent does the position have the authority to make decisions?
5. What type of guidance is provided by others and how often is the guidance provided?
6. To what extent are the job tasks circumscribed by close supervision and/or rules?
7. What are the most difficult and complex tasks of the job?

8. What type of training and experience is needed to perform the job?

9. Are there any special or unusual demands in the job (e.g., travel, unusual hours, special responsibilities)?

10. To whom does the position communicate regularly both inside and outside the organization and how often do the communications occur?

11. What type of equipment is used in the job?

12. Are there unpleasant or difficult working conditions that must be dealt with (e.g., cold, heat, dust, odors)?

13. What types of hazards are involved in the job (e.g., exposure to disease, asbestos, hazardous machinery, tools)?

14. How much physical effort is required, and if considerable physical effort is required, how often and for what duration (is it mostly sitting, standing, lifting, climbing)?

15. How many and what type of positions are supervised by this position?

16. To whom does the position report, how often, and in what way?

17. What types of resources (e.g., financial and physical) are controlled by the position?

When evaluating candidates, they should not only possess the requisite skills to perform the job, they must also fit into the broader demands of the position as suggested by these questions. For example, if a job is placed in a work setting in which the work is primarily unsupervised, it is essential to select candidates who not only possess the requisite skills to perform the basic tasks, but who also have sufficient self-motivation and dependability to work with little or no supervision. The key to good hiring is a thorough and realistic appraisal of the character of the job, as well as the specific tasks to be performed. Interviews conducted on the basis of specific job criteria have been found to be more accurate than when the job is poorly understood.[1]

STEP 2: ESTABLISH A STRUCTURE FOR THE INTERVIEW PROCESS

Often, the employer has already established procedures for the interview process. Whatever the situation, a structure for the interview should be established so that interviewers can be chosen and briefed.

Whenever possible select a structured interview:
Research indicates clearly that "structured" interviews are much more reliable than unstructured ones.[2] Structured interviews involve the construction of set questions which are asked of all candidates. Unstructured interviews allow the candidate to wander; in such a situation information which is irrelevant or even unlawful can be provided inadvertently. Structured interviews, on the other hand, collect similar information from all candidates. This allows that all relevant information can be obtained and that candidates can be compared. This does not mean, however, that every question asked must be the same for each candidate, only that the same areas should be covered. For example, unique aspects of a candidate's work background can be explored by probing questions in this area.

Whenever possible use a panel interview: As with a structured interview, there is good evidence that the use of multiple interviewers is preferable to a single interview.[3] This will be discussed in more detail below.

STEP 3: IDENTIFY THE INDIVIDUALS WHO WILL REVIEW MATERIALS, INTERVIEW AND EVALUATE CANDIDATES

In many cases, especially for lower-level positions, only one individual may be responsible for reviewing applications and evaluating candidates for hire. Often this is the immediate supervisor. Generally, this is the best choice in that there is evidence that the most accurate evaluations are by individuals who are knowledgeable about the work to be performed.[4] Immediate supervisors are usually aware of the specific job tasks to be performed and are also cognizant of the work environment and conditions to which the new employee will be subjected. Although immediate supervisors may be most knowledgeable about the job, it is wise for at least one additional individual to be involved in the selection process even for lower-level positions. This may be the director in a small library because the director is still ultimately responsible for everyone who works in a library. In a larger library it may be an upper-level supervisor or member of the personnel department.

For positions of greater responsibility, especially in medium- to large-size libraries, it is advisable to have several individuals directly involved in the evaluation of application materials and the interview process. Having multiple evaluators has at least two advantages:

1. It decreases the chance that a single individual's bias will be imposed and allows for the expression of multiple points of view.
2. The increased variety of perspectives can enrich the amount of information obtained in the interview.

Generally in larger organizations, those selected to evaluate the interviewee should include the immediate supervisor, an upper-level manager, and a personnel administrator. In any case, among the interviewers should be individuals who know the job to be performed. The greater the knowledge of the job, the more accurate the evaluation.

A common strategy used in academia or for higher-level positions in public libraries is a variation of multiple interviewers—the Search Committee. The responsibility of the Search Committee is often broader than that of multiple interviewers in that the members of the committee are often involved in early hiring stages, such as the recruitment and advertising aspects. Applications are often sent directly to the head of the Search Committee who distributes materials to the members for their evaluation. Search committees have several distinct advantages:

- They increase the involvement and participation of a greater number of staff, which in turn permits a greater diversity of individuals involved throughout the process. People with different points of view broaden and deepen the deliberative process.

- They provide a political advantage because individuals from various strata of the organization are often involved. The candidate selected from such a process may have greater legitimacy and thus a better chance at being effective from the start.

- They can provide for racial, ethnic, and gender diversity which may provide support in case of a discrimination challenge.

- They can serve as a form of staff development as the participants learn more about the organization, its philosophy, needs, policies, and practices.

Although there are distinct advantages to such committees, employers who use them should be aware of several important issues:

1. The selection of who serves on Search Committees can be a delicate political matter. Egos can become involved. The individual selecting the members of the committee should consider:

   - The individual's knowledge of the job to be filled.

   - Whether the individual can serve effectively on the committee in terms of completing work and interacting cooperatively with other members.

   - Whether the individual is fair-minded and can evaluate candidates objectively even when they may have a personal interest in advancing a particular candidate.

   - Whether the individual can see the interests of the organization as a whole as well as serve as a representative of an important interest in the organization (e.g., peers, management, minorities).

   A similar issue is selecting the individual who heads the Search Committee. Again, attention must not only be paid to political issues, but the ability of the chair to be an impartial and tactful leader.

2. The use of search committees is expensive. Often such committees may consist of four or five members all of whom must be given time to meet, review applications, interview, and make selection decisions.

3. The deliberative process can be complex. A method must be selected which takes into account each person's point of view, but which also can aggregate the opinions of each member into a final decision. This involves developing a systematic process of ranking and/or scoring candidates.

4. The charge of the committee must be clear including what the outcome of the committee's decision should be. Many search committees, for example, are responsible only for recommending two or three candidates; in other cases, the committee makes the final decision.

5. Training must be provided. Research has shown that training improves the performance of interviewers.[5] As a general practice, the library should offer good interview training to all individuals who are likely to be involved in the hiring process. In regard to a specific hire, each member will bring to the committee varying degrees of knowledge concerning hiring policies and practices. An orientation session reviewing the legal issues and institutional policies and practices must be conducted for each hiring process. The training should emphasize the importance of the hiring process and of each member's role in that process.

STEP 4: ESTABLISH A SCHEDULE FOR THE HIRING PROCESS

The hiring process can become quite protracted even in the best of circumstance. A hiring schedule can assist the selectors in expediting the process. Keep in mind that when hiring decisions are delayed the employer can lose valuable individuals. This wastes the time of those involved in the selection process and may create an impression among staff that the employer is inefficient. Hiring schedules should be as tight as possible but must be realistic. Time must be allowed for all aspects of the hiring process.

STEP 5: PREPARE JOB EVALUATION CRITERIA

All staff involved in the hiring of a particular position should have a good idea of what they are looking for in a candidate. To accomplish this, each selector should carefully review the job description with special attention to the job tasks to be performed and the required knowledge, skill, and abilities for the position. In addition, the selectors should reach a consensus on the character of the job as defined by such job factors as those above. Finally, the selectors should also consider any other job related traits that they consider important for a candidate to possess. These traits may be less tangible and more difficult to measure, but they should not be ignored. Among the traits of good employees are the following:[6]

Ability to communicate: To speak and write well.

Ambition: The desire to progress in the organization and profession.

Attention to personal appearance: Understanding what is appropriate, business-like attire.

Commitment to the organization and the profession: The desire to remain and make extra efforts for the library and to develop professionally.

Consciousness: Exhibiting responsibility and dedication to work.

Cooperativeness: The willingness to deal constructively and positively with co-workers and others.

Creativity: The capacity to propose new solutions and see problems and issues in new ways.

Empathy: The ability to put themselves in anothers place.

Good attitude: The desire to look at the workplace in a positive way and to view problems as challenges.

Good health: The ability to work vigorously and regularly.

Honesty: The desire to act ethically and lawfully in all instances.

Intelligence: The possession of the intellectual skills to perform the job well.

Maturity: The ability to choose appropriate courses of action based on experience and good judgement.

Motivation: The desire to work hard and persist in their tasks until they are completed.

Patience: The propensity to act only after all information is available.

Reliability: The propensity to be consistent in attendance and performance.

Respect for authority: The willingness to obey normal and reasonable commands of those in authority.

Of course, only the perfect employee possesses all these characteristics in ample supply, but these traits should not be ignored in the hiring process. With proper questioning during the interview and thorough reference checking, many of these traits or lack thereof may become evident.

The criteria established by the selectors should focus on the knowledge, skills, and abilities necessary to perform the job well.

This criteria might be weighted depending on which aspects of the job are most important. After a thorough discussion of the criteria for selection, the process of reviewing applications and resumes can begin.

STEP 6: REVIEW RESUMES AND APPLICATION FORMS

Job selectors usually have two basic sources of information prior to a job interview: the resume (including cover letter) and job application. A cover letter may sometimes be especially telling regarding the care taken in its preparation. Letters that are poorly typed, have been sloppily corrected, or are unnecessarily wordy or confusing may be an indicator that the applicant is unacceptable. It is appropriate that interviewers review the resume or cover letter, but the selectors should place special emphasis on the information in a well-prepared application form. It is here that pertinent information is presented in a consistent fashion. It may be a good idea to *prepare a checklist or evaluation form* to reflect key aspects of the selection criteria, which would permit the selectors to note briefly for each applicant the extent to which the applicant possesses the desired work experience, educational background and other appropriate knowledge, skill, and abilities.

Aside from looking for the necessary knowledge, skills, and ability of the applicant, several other questions should be asked when examining the application form or resume. These include the following:

- Is the resume or application form readable and/or well written? Are there signs of carelessness such as misspellings or poorly constructed sentences?
- Did the applicant provide complete information? Are all the questions answered? Are full names, addresses, and dates of employment provided?
- Are there job gaps? Are there long periods of time which remain unexplained? Is there any indication of what the individual was doing between jobs?

- Has the applicant held many jobs over a short period of time?
- Are the reasons for leaving jobs missing, or do the explanations for leaving seem unclear or evasive?

Few applications are flawless in preparation and candidates should not necessarily be excluded merely because of job gaps or incomplete information. But these may be subjects for subsequent questioning if an interview is recommended.

Based on the resume and/or application, the selectors should choose the most qualified applicants for interview. The number of individuals interviewed depends on many factors including the number of strong candidates for the position, the amount of money available to conduct interviews, and the amount of time available to conduct interviews.

STEP 7: INFORM PROSPECTIVE INTERVIEWEES

Candidates who are selected for interview should generally be informed by a telephone call. This is an opportunity to get a first impression of the candidate. If possible, the candidate should be given optional times for interview, but this may be severely limited based on the time constraints of the hiring process and on the selectors' other responsibilities. In many cases, the candidate is local and there is little need to provide directions and additional information. However, if the candidate is traveling a long distance, the candidate should be given directions and/or provided a map through the mail. In addition, such candidates should be informed if travel and other costs will be assumed by the employer, and if the employer will make the necessary arrangements for accommodations and transportation. All this information should be confirmed in a follow-up letter. For high-level positions, the employer should also prepare a packet of materials concerning the library and the geographic area and send it to the candidate.

For internal candidates, a face-to-face meeting is appropriate, giving the employee the time and place of the interview and any other informational materials that may have a direct bearing on the content of the interview. This can be followed by a letter confirming the information provided in the meeting.

STEP 8: PREPARE AN INTERVIEW DAY TIME SCHEDULE

The preparation of an interview schedule is only necessary when a position is sufficiently important that many appointments may be necessary for the candidate. This is most common in administrative or management positions in academic and in administrative positions in larger public libraries.

When a candidate must meet several individuals, there is considerable likelihood that without a schedule, some important contact will either be missed or inappropriately squeezed into an abbreviated time slot. The interview schedule provides structure for both the candidate and employer. The candidate is made aware of who he or she will meet and when; the selectors are able to determine when it is time to terminate contact with the candidate and where to take the candidate when time is up.

The schedule should begin with the earliest point of contact (e.g., picking up the candidate at the airport or meeting for breakfast). It should indicate in specified time blocks exactly when various individuals are given the opportunity to interview the candidate. If the candidate is scheduled to be with the employer for at least a day, time should be formally scheduled for breaks, lunch, and dinner. The schedule should be prepared well in advance and sent to the candidate and any individuals who will be involved in the interview process.

A variety of options are available in designing an interview day. Obviously, a formal interview with a search committee or designated selector(s) must be part of the process. Other possible contacts may include:

1. meetings with the director or key administrator(s) if they are not already part of the interview team,
2. meetings with peers or subordinates, and
3. meeting with the personnel department regarding institutional policies, benefits, etc.

STEP 9: PREPARE QUESTIONS FOR THE INTERVIEW

Question preparation is a critical part of the hiring process. It is through the questions and the candidate's responses to these questions that the selectors are able to determine, in large part, the candidates suitability for the job. It is tempting to ask a wide variety of questions, and the selectors should not be shy about asking challenging and probing ones. But it is also important before formulating questions to understand the purpose of the interview. Eder provides an excellent definition of the interview:

> The employment interview is defined as a face-to-face exchange of job-relevant information between organizational representatives and a job applicant with the overall organizational goal of attracting, selecting, and retaining a highly competent workforce.[7]

Although asking questions is a critical part of the process, the interview is also an important opportunity to create a positive image to the candidate and to provide information to the interviewee and answer questions that the interviewee may have. Good candidates will judge the organization by the manner and type of questions asked, just as the organization judges the candidate by his or her responses.

The questions should focus on those aspects of the individual's background that deal with the knowledge, skill and ability to perform the job for which the candidate is applying. Extraneous, non-job-related questions should be avoided. The interview is not a personal conversation, it is a business function. Its primary purpose is to predict the success of the employee in the new job.

The selection and formulation of questions must be tailored specifically to the requirements of the particular job. Collecting irrelevant or non-job-related information is inappropriate and should be avoided.

There are various types of questions that can be asked of candidates. Generally they fall into two categories: closed-ended and open-ended questions.

Closed-ended questions usually require short, factual, or yes-and-no responses. Their purpose is usually to gather very specific information (e.g., "Are you willing to work full time?").

Open-ended questions allow the candidate to talk at length, exploring the candidate's attitudes, opinions and job values (e.g., "Why have you applied for this position?"). A special type of open-ended question is called the *projective question*, which will be discussed in detail below.

The approach one takes in questioning a candidate is extremely important. Some interviewers ask very general or vague questions about the candidate's educational or work background. For example, the interviewer may ask: "Describe your ideal supervisor." Although such a request may have merit, a more effective approach would be to determine the candidate's attitude toward supervision by specifically probing the individuals reaction to past and current supervisors. One might, for example, ask "Describe your last supervisor. What did you like about his or her supervisory approach? What did you dislike?" The technique of deriving job-related information about a candidate by probing previous educational and work experience is called *anchoring*. Underlying this technique is the premise that performance in previous jobs is a stronger indicator of future performance than an interviewee's general remarks based on a general question. Anchoring has several distinct advantages: (1) the queries are job related; (2) the candidate discusses what is known (the past) rather than speculating on a general idea or about the future; (3) the candidate is less able to "snow" the interviewers with glittering generalities; (4) many statements made about previous work are often verifiable, if it is necessary to check with a previous employer or educational institution. A final advantage is that it enables interviewers to ground their impressions in specific statements from the candidate. It is not uncommon that interviewers get a subjective impression of a candidate but have difficulty proving this impression. When an interviewer begins to get a feeling about a candidate, the interviewer should try to anchor this impression through questioning about previous work. For example, if an interviewer believes that the candidate may have trouble getting along with people the interviewer might probe the candidate's perception of co-workers in previous jobs, or whether the candidate preferred to work in team situations or to work alone. (The interviewer may discover communication problems or a preference for working alone.) If the interviewer can anchor subjective impressions in objective statements made by the candidate, the employer is in a much stronger position when making a final job selection.

JOB-RELATED AREAS

The job-related areas for questioning can be broken down into a variety of segments. One way of looking at them is to separate the questioning into the following categories: (1) general questions; (2) questions concerning educational background; and (3) questions concerning work background and experience.

General Questions: There are a variety of areas which the employer must explore that is related to the job and the workplace as a whole. These questions are not necessarily seeking specific information about the knowledge, skills, and abilities of the candidate, but explore general motivations as well as whether the candidate and the demands of the organization fit. Such questions explore quite different aspects of the candidate and are not asked at any given time. Different ones may be asked at appropriate times throughout the interview.

Sample questions

1. Why have you applied for this position?
2. Given this position's work schedule, would you have any difficulty with consistent attendance?
3. If we had two openings, one part-time and one full-time, which one would you prefer?
4. Do you have a specific salary requirement?
5. If you were offered the position, when could you start working?
6. Do you have any questions concerning this position or the organization?
7. Do you have any additional information that you would like to provide us that would help us to make a decision?

Education And Training: A basic aspect of assessing a candidate's suitability is matching the education and training of the individual to the specific job. Questions should not only concern themselves with facts (what courses were taken) but also with the ability of the candidate to determine how the knowledge gained would be applied to the position. In addition, the candidate should be asked to evaluate her educational strengths and weaknesses.

Sample Questions

1. What courses did you take in school that would help you to perform the job for which you are applying?

2. In what courses did you perform the best? What accounts for your strong performance in this area? Where would you say you are weakest in terms of your course work? How would you explain this?

3. Are you particularly proud of any particular project or activity in which you were involved while you were at school? Tell me about it.

4. Did you receive special vocational or technical training that would help you to perform your job? What training did you receive and how would you apply it?

5. Have you taken any continuing education courses that would help you do your work? What courses did you take and how would you apply them?

6. Did you receive any special training in the military that would help you perform in this job? What type of training would apply to this position?

Work Experience: For most positions, work experience is the single most important area to be examined. Work-related questions must probe not only the facts regarding specific tasks performed, but attitudes toward the work itself, the working conditions and supervision. When probing work experience, it is especially important to examine how the individual fits in regard to the broader aspects of the job (e.g., level of decision-making, freedom of action, job complexity).

Tasks: A key component of job success and satisfaction is the ability of the employee to perform well the tasks of the job itself. The interviewer must determine if the candidate's previous job tasks were related to the tasks to be performed and if so, was the employee satisfied performing those tasks. For each current and previous position of interest, the interviewer might probe with the following questions.

Sample Questions

1. What were the specific tasks of your job?

2. On which tasks did you spend the greatest amount of time? (What percent of the time did you spend on each task?)

3. Which tasks did you enjoy the most? Why?

4. Which tasks did you enjoy the least? Why?

5. Was the position full- or part-time? If part-time, how many hours a week?

6. Did the position involve public contact? What percent of the time?

7. Describe a difficult situation you have had with a member of the public. How did you handle it? Were you satisfied with the result? How might you have handled the situation differently?

8. Describe your strengths in working with the public. Can you think of specific situations in the past where these strength were used in your work? Describe a couple of these situations.

9. Describe a project or achievement in your last job about which you are most proud?

Schedule: Many library positions require considerable flexibility in work scheduling. The interviewer must examine the candidate's previous work schedules, consistency in meeting these schedules, and scheduling preferences.

Sample Questions

1. Describe your current work schedule (or your most recent work schedule). Was this schedule satisfactory or would you have preferred a different schedule? What would your preferred schedule be today?

2. Were you left in charge when your supervisor was gone? (If yes, why do you think you were given this responsibility?) How did you feel about being left in charge?

3. Did you have to fill in for absent employees or for employees on vacation? How did you feel about this?

4. Did you have previous problems in meeting your work schedules? Were you ever disciplined for inability to meet a regular work schedule?

Attitude toward supervisors: There is considerable evidence that an employee's level of job satisfaction is heavily affected by the immediate supervisor.[8] Different individuals prefer different types of supervisory styles. It is important to explore what type of supervision the candidate prefers and how the candidate has dealt with supervisors in the past.

Sample Questions

1. Describe your work relationship with your current immediate supervisor. What factors are most important in affecting your attitude toward this supervisor?

2. If we contacted your immediate supervisor, what would she say about you?

3. Describe the things you like about your supervisor? Describe the things you dislike? Why?

Supervisory experience: Exploring supervisory experience is important when the position open requires supervisory responsibilities. When a candidate indicates supervisory experience, it is very important to define what is meant. For some, supervision merely means scheduling employees; for others it may imply the entire gamut of supervisory practices such as hiring, evaluation, discipline, termination, and training. The interviewer must probe carefully to secure precise information about supervision.

Sample Questions

1. Did your position involve supervision?

2. How many individuals did you supervise at any one time?

3. Were they full or part time? (How many of each?)

4. What types of positions did they hold (clerical, professional)?

5. What were your supervisory responsibilities? Did you hire, evaluate, train, discipline, terminate, schedule these employees?

6. What characteristics did you look for in a new employee? What questions would you ask to evaluate these characteristics?

7. How did you prepare for giving a performance evaluation to a subordinate?

8. Have you ever conducted a difficult or substandard performance evaluation? Think of your most difficult. How did you prepare for it? Did the employee's performance improve? Would you handle it differently now? In what way?

9. Have you had to discipline or terminate? How did you prepare for this? Would you handle it differently today? In what way?

Work Environment: Each library has its own special environment. Perhaps it is extremely busy, perhaps the clientele is very demanding or poorly educated requiring considerable patience. The workplace may be crowded, aging, and poorly equipped, or it may be highly automated demanding high levels of flexibility in regard to training and retraining. Employers must realistically determine the work environment into which the candidate would be placed and determine if the candidate will be responsive in such an environment.

Sample Questions

1. Describe your work environment in your last job. What did you specifically like and dislike?

2. How did you handle any dissatisfaction with the work environment?

3. Describe your ideal work setting.

Reasons for Leaving: The most delicate area that the interviewer is likely to probe is the reasons why the candidate left previous positions, or why the candidate wishes to leave his or her present position. Often candidates are vague about their reasons for leaving. One may hear "personal reasons" as a common response. It is vital to get a detailed explanation as to why individuals have left their previous employers. They may indicate incompatibilities with certain work environments, or difficulties working with staff or supervisors. It may indicate weaknesses in job attitudes and disposition. On the other hand, reasons for leaving may have positive implications. It may reveal a desire for career development and a clear set of career goals. It may indicate a motivation for increased challenge.

Although clear and direct, the question, "Why did you leave your last position?" might be threatening to a candidate. A less direct possible alternative approach might be to follow a discussion of the previous job with the comment, "and then you left this position?" Such an approach invites the candidate to discuss the transition from one employer to another in a less threatening way. However, if such a technique does not work, the interviewer must probe the reasons for leaving directly. Certain specific aspects of the employment separation must be explored including whether the separation was voluntary or involuntary. For example, the interviewer must not be satisfied with the response, "I resigned," until it is clear whether the resignation was requested or voluntary.

Sample Questions

1. Why did you leave your last position?
2. Did you leave on your own accord or did your employer ask you to leave?
3. Can you discuss with me the reasons why your employer asked that you leave?
4. Can you describe the relationship with your supervisor when you left?
5. Can you describe the relationship with your co-workers or subordinates when you left?
6. If we contacted your immediate supervisor or employer, what would she say about your reason for leaving?

Projective or Situational Questions: One questioning technique sometimes used by interviewers is called projective questioning. Such questions pose a situation to the candidate and require the candidate to analyze the situation and identify what action she should take and why. Projective questions are intended to explore a candidate's job values or ability to resolve management and professional problems and take appropriate actions. Although projective questions can be useful in the interview setting, certain specific conditions should be met before using such questions:

- The situation provided must be similar to ones actually encountered in the specific job for which the candidate has applied.

- The situation must be of sufficient importance that it is a relevant job-related concern.
- The selectors must set in advance a basic criteria for evaluating the response given by the candidate. This may include assigning points to certain types of responses.

Projective Questions

1. If a patron became angry at you because of a library policy, how would you handle the situation?
2. If a patron slammed a library book on the counter and said, "How can the library buy this type of obscene trash!", how would you handle the situation?
3. If a patron came to you and said a man had just made lewd remarks to her, how would you handle the situation?
4. If a staff member came to you (as a supervisor) and said that another staff member is being rude to patrons fairly regularly, how would you handle the situation?

STEP 10: REVIEW FACTORS THAT AFFECT THE INTERVIEW JUDGMENTS OF SELECTORS

The interviewing process, even when carefully structured, is a distinctly human process. Both the interviewers and the candidates bring with them their own values, attitudes, predispositions, family, educational, and work backgrounds. Each interview is therefore a product of an interaction between these factors and produces the chemistry of the job interview. There is nothing intrinsically wrong with this. The problem arises when the decision-making process is tainted with considerations that are not relevant to determining the ability of the candidates to perform the job. It is impossible to eliminate these considerations, but there is good evidence that well-informed and trained interviewers are less likely to impose their biases.[9] As part of this informing process interviewers should regularly be made aware that their judgements can be affected inappropriately. Among the factors that affect interview judgements are the following:[10]

1. Interview decisions are made very early in the interview process. There is evidence that decisions about an interview are often made in the first few minutes of an interview. This is far too early to make a good judgement in most cases and the interviewer must be scrupulous about giving the interviewee a chance. Many candidates are very nervous at the beginning of an interview and their behavior may become more natural as the interview proceeds.

2. Greater weight is placed on negative information than on positive information. When a candidate volunteers information which reflects poorly on her, such as being terminated, or having past emotional problems, interviewers have a tendency to place greater emphasis on this information than on a positive response. Although negative information must be taken into account in any interview, the information must be properly balanced with positive aspects of the candidate.

3. The personal feelings of the interviewers toward the candidate weigh more heavily than they should in the interview process. Of particular importance is what is known as candidate likability. If an interviewer likes a candidate, she has a tendency to overlook the negative aspects of the interviewee and emphasize the positive. The opposite may be true if the interviewer does not like the candidate. Although it is important that a candidate be able to get along with other employees, a candidate's knowledge, skill, and ability must play the critical role in the decision-making process, not whether the candidate is liked by the interviewer. Consequently interviewers must be particularly conscious to make sure that this does not weigh unduly in the hiring decision.

4. Interviewees' non-verbal behaviors such as eye contact, neutral facial expressions, holding the head still instead of nodding during conversation, and low energy significantly influence the interviewer's judgement. Even such things as perfume scents, articulation, pauses in speech, and handshakes have been known to affect

interviewer judgment. Although personal mannerisms may play some role in the interviewer's judgments, the evaluator must emphasize the suitability of the candidate in terms of a match between the job and the candidate's knowledge, skill and abilities.

5. Females tend to receive lower ratings than males. There is no research in the library profession regarding how interviewers evaluate males and females, but research outside the profession reveals a disturbing propensity of evaluators to give lower evaluations to women than to men. Part of this may be the fact that the successful performance of women tends to be attributed more often to luck or circumstances, while men's success is more often attributed to effort and ability. Under these circumstances, even strong female candidates will be seen as less able than their male counterparts.[11]

6. Attractive candidates of either sex receive higher ratings. Interviewers, like other humans beings, respond positively to their own society's view of what is considered beautiful. Candidates who are perceived as being physically attractive receive higher ratings than those who are not. Because there is no relationship between physical attractiveness and job performance in most positions, this factor must be eliminated in the deliberative process.

7. Individuals with disabilities are given lower evaluations than individuals without disabilities. Unfortunately, individuals who appear to us as different tend to make us feel uncomfortable. This translates into lower evaluations in the interview. This is a troubling finding not only because it is unfair, but because it is a clear violation of current federal law. If a candidate could demonstrate that the disability was the actual reason for a poor interview evaluation, the employer could be subjected to substantial liabilities. A more detailed discussion dealing with individuals with disabilities can be found in Chapter 7.

Aside from these factors, there are several other issues with which the interviewer must deal.

Contrast effect: Contrast effect is related to the order in which candidates are interviewed. For example, when candidates are being interviewed within a short time period, there is evidence that the success or failure of the first interview affects the judgment of the subsequent candidate. If the first candidate performs very well, then the second candidate is rated lower than he or she would otherwise be rated if the first candidate had not been interviewed. Conversely, if the first candidate performs poorly in the interview, the second candidate will be rated higher than he or would otherwise have been rated. Interviewers must be conscious of this effect, especially when the interviews take place close to one another.

Confirmatory judgment: Interviewers usually have some idea or impression of a candidate before she is interviewed. This idea may be based on a review of the resume and application, on references, or personal experience. Regardless of the basis of the knowledge, there is evidence that interviewers construct their questions and interpret answers in a way that confirms their pre-interview impressions of the candidate. If the interviewer has a positive pre-interview impression, then questions will be asked to elicit positive responses.[12] If the impression is negative, then the opposite will occur. Interviewers must be especially sensitive to the fact that even when the same questions are asked, the phrasing and emphasis can elicit different responses. Questions phrased in a negative or threatening manner may well elicit very different responses.

Interviewer's non-verbal behavior: Interviewers should also be aware that the performance of the interviewee is not entirely the responsibility of the candidate. The performance of the interviewer can seriously affect the performance of the interviewee. If an interviewer provides an open and friendly environment for the candidate, the interviewee is more likely to relax and provide more information. Interviewers who clearly make disapproving gestures or remarks, or show hostility or disinterest are likely to foreclose the possibility of a fruitful and informative interview.

The interviewer's behavior may also have important implications for the organization because the perception of the interviewer can shape the candidate's judgment of the worthiness of the organization. If a candidate is treated professionally and honestly, the candidate is more likely to view the employer in a positive light. This is especially critical if the candidate is interviewing with other employers. The candidate's impression of the employer at the interview may substantially affect his or her job choice.

STEP 11: REVIEW INAPPROPRIATE AREAS FOR QUESTIONING

When developing questions for an interview, there are several types of questions that should be avoided (see Appendix E). First, the interviewer should keep in mind that he or she is in a position of considerable power. Candidates tend to feel nervous and vulnerable in such situations. This is reasonable in that the selectors have the power to affect the candidate's future employment. Under these circumstances, some interviewers probe into personal or private topics which have no relationship to the individual's ability to perform the job. Such a tactic is unethical and should be strictly prohibited. A second area that should be avoided is any query that could be construed as having a discriminatory impact or intent. Such questions may make the employer especially vulnerable to legal liabilities and public embarrassment.

Among the questions that should *not* be asked are those concerning:

Age: Questions about age are usually prohibited unless there is a special reason related to law. For example, the employer can only query whether the individual is under 18 due to child labor laws that may affect the employability of the candidate.

Disability: With the passage of the Americans with Disabilities Act almost all queries prior to selection regarding a candidate's disabilities are prohibited. If the candidate volunteers information about a disability, the employer can inquire into the nature of the accommodation required to permit the candidate to perform the essential functions of the job. Otherwise, questions concerning physical and mental health may not be asked.

Marital status/Family status: Questions concerning marital status, number of children, childcare arrangements or pregnancy are not permitted. Usually, such queries are made out of a concern that the candidate may not be able to meet a regular work schedule. If this is the reason, the employer may discuss the regular schedule for the position and ask the candidate if there is any reason why the candidate could not meet such a schedule.

Race/Color/Ethnicity: Questions concerning a person's national or racial background are prohibited.

Religion: A candidate's religion is not an appropriate subject for inquiry including which religious holidays are observed. The focus of the employer's inquiry should be on meeting a regular work schedule, not on religious beliefs. If a candidate indicates a problem with working certain days because of religious beliefs, the employer must review the responsibilities for reasonable accommodation before making a final selection decision.

STEP 12: ENSURE A PRIVATE AREA FOR INTERVIEWING

Locating a private area in which the interview is conducted is important for a variety of reasons. First, it permits the selectors to listen to the candidate's responses without distraction. Second, it sends a message to the candidate that the interview is important and deserves the full attention of the selectors and the employer. The arrangement of the interview room itself may be limited due to physical constraints. If give and take is to be encouraged, it is best to have the selectors and the candidate seated around a table, rather than the selectors sitting at a panel with the candidate seated in front of the panel.

STEP 13: APPOINT AN INTERVIEWER-IN-CHARGE

One of the interviewers should be assigned the task of controlling the interview. This individual may be responsible for greeting and introducing the candidate, providing information about the interview process and closing the interview. This individual should also be responsible for keeping the interview on track, for moving the interview along, and for monitoring to ensure that only appropriate questions are being asked. In larger organizations, this might be an individual from the personnel or human resources department.

STEP 14: WELCOME THE CANDIDATE AND INTRODUCE THE PROCESS

The interview situation is an especially stressful one for most job candidates and the candidate will not know exactly what to do. One of the interviewers should be assigned to greet the candidate either at the entrance to the library or at a designated location. A friendly greeting should help put the candidate at ease. When entering the interview area, the candidate should be introduced to all the selectors including what position each interviewer fills in the library, then guided to the appropriate place to sit. Some small talk for a very brief period is permissible to put the candidate at ease.

Once the candidate is seated comfortably, one of the interviewers (selected in advance) should be responsible for providing an introduction to the interview process. For example, the interviewer might indicate that it is a structured interview setting, that different interviewers will ask different questions, and that the interviewers will be taking copious notes. The candidate should be assured that if a question is unclear, that he or she should feel comfortable asking for clarification. It may also be a good time to indicate to the candidate that he or she will be allowed to ask any questions they have at the end of the interview.

STEP 15: CONDUCT THE INTERVIEW

Using the questions prepared for the interview, the candidate should be asked about his or her knowledge, skill, and ability to perform the job. Among the issues to keep in mind while conducting the interview are:

Give the candidate time to think and talk: An interview is not an opportunity for the interviewers to make speeches, reminisce, or tell stories about their experience in library work; it is intended to elicit information from the candidate. The candidate should be given plenty of time to think about responses and to reflect on her or his answers. From time to time, especially talkative candidates might have to be redirected by the interviewer in charge, but generally the more a candidate talks, the more information that is obtained.

Maintain a positive attitude: Because the attitude of the interviewer(s) plays a substantial role in the interviewee's responses, it is critical that the interview be conducted in as non-threatening a manner as possible. Although delicate areas, such as reasons for leaving, may have to be probed, these questions should be asked in a non-judgmental fashion.

Take notes: Notes taken in the interview are an important record of the deliberative process. Such notes have at least three purposes:

1. Notes serve as support for the memory. Although interviewers may believe that they remember what a candidate says, the passage of time can substantially blur the recollection.
2. Notes improve the ability of interviewers to compare the qualifications and abilities of candidates.

3. Notes provide important documentation in case a hiring decision is challenged by an unsuccessful candidate. Interviewers should be aware that the notes they take can be used as evidence in an administrative hearing or court room so it is vital that only job-related information be maintained in these notes.

Notes should be taken while the interview is being conducted. This sometimes results in losing eye contact with the interviewee and it is important to re-establish this contact as soon as possible. There also may be occasions when the interviewer may want to briefly delay taking notes. This includes moments when the candidate may be volunteering sensitive, negative information. For example, if an individual was involuntarily terminated from a position, it may be best to listen sympathetically while the candidate is explaining the situation, and then make notes soon thereafter. This should diminish the chance that the candidate feels the information had undue weight.

Ask only job-related questions: Any and all interviewers should be especially careful to avoid any inquiries that are not job-related. The farther afield an interview goes, the greater the potential that the candidate might suspect that subjective criteria are being imposed.

Give the candidate an opportunity to ask questions: Once the interviewers have asked their questions, the candidates should be able to ask whatever questions they wish to. It is wise to write down the questions asked and a summary of the answers given not only as a documentary record, but because the questions asked by the candidate may indicate the amount of "homework" done on the organization, personal priorities, and analytical skills.

Close the interview: After the candidate has asked questions, he or she should be given an opportunity to make any other additional comments or volunteer any other additional information that would help the selectors make their decision. After the candidate has finished with these comments, the individual in charge of the interview should inform the candidate of the next step in the process. If the interview is the final step, the candidate should be informed when a hiring decision is likely to be made and how they will be informed. The candidate should then be thanked for participating in the interview and escorted to their next destination.

Summarize notes: After the interview, the selectors should summarize their notes indicating the candidate's strengths and weaknesses. This may prove very useful, especially if there are relatively lengthy gaps between candidate interviews.

Review for possible problems: After the interviews have been conducted, it is good to examine the process to see if there are any notable problems. Below is a summary of possible reasons for failures in the interview process:

1. Failure to have a clear idea of the job to be filled, or a written description of the job. This results in an unfocused interview and will confuse the selection decision because the qualifications of the candidates can not be compared against a set of job tasks.

2. Failure to focus questions on the related knowledge, skill, and abilities required for the job. This will also make it impossible to compare the candidates' skills with the job tasks. It may also make the library culpable to charges of discrimination.

3. Failure to prepare for the interview and/or review carefully the application form and resume. This may waste library resources because unqualified or otherwise inappropriate candidates are invited for interview. Similarly, poor preparation can lead to a poorly focused interview and an impression on the candidate's part of an unprofessional organization.

4. Failure to filter preconceived notions about the candidate. This adversely affects the interviewer's ability to pick the best qualified candidate thus damaging the library's productivity. Similarly, it could lead to charges of discrimination if the preconceptions deal with race, religion, or other characteristics protected by law.

5. Failure to make the candidate comfortable so that free expression is encouraged. This results in inaccurate or insufficient information in the interview, and gives the interviewee a poor impression of the library.

6. Failure to conduct a structured interview in which the same basic information is gathered from all candidates. This severely limits the ability to compare candidates and gives the impression of confusion to the interviewee.

7. Failure to ask questions in a positive way and in a similar manner to each candidate. This casts an unnecessarily negative character to interviewee responses and may give the interviewee an impression that a prejudgment has been made. It also reduces the communicativeness of the candidate.

8. Failure to probe sensitive but important job-related areas. This leads to loss of vital information and the hire of an individual who may be inappropriate or harmful to the library.

9. Failure to evaluate responses in a similar fashion. This leads to the unfair elimination of qualified candidates and the hire of less qualified ones.

10. Failure to listen carefully to the candidate and to take detailed notes in the interview. Candidates cannot be adequately compared unless the information is absorbed by the interviewer. Similarly, without written notes, it is hard to document a job selection when the decision is challenged.

11. Failure to abide by Equal Employment Opportunity laws and regulations. This subjects the organization to unnecessary and considerable liabilities. It also represents unethical and unprofessional conduct.

12. Failure to provide privacy and a comfortable setting for the candidate. This seriously limits the chance that the candidate will be expansive and interferes with the interviewer's ability to question and absorb important information.

13. Failure to give the applicant an opportunity to ask questions. This affects the applicant's ability to assess the suitability of the job. Consequently, the candidate may determine that she does not want a position with the library.

14. Failure to wait until the interview is over *before* drawing conclusions about the candidate. This leads to incorrect

judgments and fails to give candidates an equal chance to convince the interviewer of their suitability.

STEP 15: OPTIONAL ACTIVITIES WHILE THE CANDIDATE IS IN THE BUILDING

Showing the candidate around: It is the practice in some organizations to give the individual a tour of the library. This also may involve meeting and talking with staff members. This gives the candidate a better idea of the actual working conditions of the organization. Although there are some advantages to this process, employers must be scrupulous about ensuring that any questions asked by staff conform to the law. There is no such thing as an informal part of the interview process and questions such as those concerning age, marital and family status, and disabilities are just as inappropriate in this setting as in the interview.

Job tests and tryouts: Although the job interview is the most common way by which employers determine the suitability of a candidate, the validity of the interview has been questioned.[13] For this reason, other techniques have been applied in business and industry to provide additional job-related information for assessing candidates. These are tests or tryouts.

There are many types of tests, but usually two are used: paper tests and work simulations. Paper tests vary widely including standardized personality, integrity and attitude tests, and tests of a candidate's knowledge of librarianship including the ability to identify popular or classic titles. Work simulations attempt to simulate the actual tasks of the job to be performed. Simple examples of work simulations would be typing tests in which the individual is expected to prepare correspondence similar to that prepared in the actual position, filing tests in which the candidate is asked to file catalog or shelf list cards, or shelving tests in which a potential shelver is asked to arrange books or numbers in the proper order. For upper-level positions, more sophisticated simulations may be involved. For example, an *in-basket test* may be used for an administrative candidate. This often involves having a stack of memos or other communications which the candidate must review and indicate the proper action to be taken. As with the use of projective questions discussed earlier, such tests require that a criteria be established in advance so that the responses of the candidates can be consistently scored and evaluated. Although the in-basket test is popular in business, research indicates that they are of only modest usefulness as a measurement.[14] Another type of simulation, more common in academic hiring, is the *presentation*. Usually a candidate is given a topic to present during a specific time period, usually between 15 minutes and one hour. Often all or selected staff, as well as the selectors, are invited to hear the presentation. In some cases, those who listen to the presentation are asked to evaluate and make comments on paper. In other cases, only the selectors actually evaluate the candidate formally. In either case, it is important that the criteria for the evaluation be job-related. If communication skills, ability to answer questions and ability to organize material are essential functions of the job, then the presentation should be evaluated on these factors.

Employers must be aware that the Equal Employment Opportunity Commissions uses a very broad definition of a job test. This means that almost any type of test or tryout used by a library employer would fall under the scrutiny of employment discrimination laws. Any test that would have the effect of disproportionately screening out minorities and other protected classes could subject the employer to considerable liabilities. If, for example, the library used a typing test, and this test led to a disproportionate number of failed tests among African-Americans than whites, the test could be construed as discriminatory, especially if an alternative method of measurement produced nondiscriminatory results. If differential results are found in a job test or tryout, the employer is required to validate the test based on the standards issued by the EEOC in the *Uniform Guidelines on Employee Selection*, and *Questions and Answers on the Uniform Guidelines on Employee Selection*. At the very least, when the employer is developing a test, it should have what is called *face validity*. Face validity means that there is an obvious relationship between the knowledge or skill being tested and the activities of the job itself. If, for example, a clerical position requires a lot of typing, then a typing test may be in order, insofar as the typing speed required is realistic in terms of the job. Setting unduly high typing standards, even when typing is required for the position, would increase the vulnerability of the employer to liability.

Because tests or tryouts should deal specifically with the job, it is also unwise to borrow other libraries' tests unless the jobs are similar.

The employer should also consider the place that a test fits into the hiring process. When test scores are given such importance that they are used to *eliminate* candidates, they must be scrupulously prepared, administered, and scored. In general, employers should be wary about using a single test to eliminate a candidate. Test-taking is as much an art as a science, and applicants who are extremely nervous or anxious may not be able to demonstrate their abilities in a single test. Remember that the test taking situation is not necessarily the same as the situation in the workplace, and people may behave differently in the normal environment of the library. A good employee could be lost if too much weight is placed on this part of the evaluation process.

In summary, if a test or tryout is given, the employer should keep in mind at least the following points:

1. The test should cover knowledge and/or skills that are important in the performance of the job.
2. The test should be carefully prepared so that it is clear.
3. The test should be administered in the same fashion and under the same conditions for each candidate.
4. Criteria for scoring and evaluating the test should be prepared in advance.
5. Each test should be scored and evaluated in the same fashion for each candidate.
6. The test should have only its due weight in the decision-making process and should not be used to exclude candidates unless it can be shown that the missing knowledge or skill is essential to perform the job.
7. The test results should be scrupulously monitored to ensure that protected classes are not being screened out.
8. Alternative testing procedures should be considered whenever there is doubt about the validity of the test or if the test appears to screen out members of protected classes.

Asking for Examples of Work: Another option for the employer is to ask the individual for examples of work performed in previous positions. A candidate for a children's position, for example, might be asked to bring in examples of materials used in programs previously conducted by the candidate. A candidate for a public relations position might be asked to supply examples of reports or informational and promotional materials created by the candidate. A director might be asked to supply previously prepared planning documents or annual reports for which the director was responsible. In each case, the same request for materials should be made of all candidates and a criteria for evaluation should be established *before* examining the material.

STEP 16: CHECKING REFERENCES

Checking references is a common, traditional, and still important activity in the hiring process. However, given the reluctance of many employers to give references these days due to potential legal liabilities, the amount of information obtained is often limited. Nonetheless, it is the employer's responsibility to try to gather as much job-related information as possible and reference checking is part of this information-gathering process.

Among the issues that must be confronted is what type of references to check. *Personal or character references* are supplied by friends and confidants of the employee. These individuals may be family members, neighbors, workmates, or clergy who are familiar with the personal habits and character of the individual. They may attest to the honesty, integrity, and personality of the candidate. However, these individuals may be unfamiliar with the work habits of the applicant. As a rule, such references are of little value in predicting job success. After all, who would provide the name of an individual who would give a poor character reference? Also, given the subjectivity of such references, it may be difficult to apply the personal remarks to the ability of the candidate to perform the job. For these reasons, requests for such references are of very limited value.

The other type of reference is the *work reference*. The names of such references may come from the candidate or from the work history on the application form. In either case, the employer should obtain written permission to obtain work references before contacting the referees. This can be accomplished on the application form in the agreement which is signed by the candidate (see Appendix D). In addition, for each employer listed on the application form, there should be a space for the applicant to indicate if the employer can be contacted for a reference. Once permission has been given, a reference should be solicited. Often candidates will hesitate to give permission to contact their current employer. Such contact, they reasonably fear, could affect the attitude of the employer. This request should be respected, and references of current employers should not be checked without express permission of the candidate. However, the employer should reserve the right to make a reference check of the current employer after an offer for hire has been made, making clear that the appointment could be withdrawn if substantial negative information was obtained.

There are usually two basic approaches to reference checking: the telephone check and the reference letter. The point at which either technique is used varies widely from the point of application to after a candidate has been selected for hire. Each technique has its advantages and disadvantages. Telephone reference checks can be done quickly, can be conducted in-depth with each party being able to ask questions and provide follow-up comments. It is more likely to produce frank and forthright comments. A disadvantage is that there is no written record except notes taken by the prospective employer. If the previous employer makes negative remarks that influence the prospective employer, the applicant may subsequently claim that the remarks were defamatory. The referee could deny making these remarks, thus exposing the employer to substantial legal liabilities. In order to improve the quality and documentation of the telephone reference process, the employer needs to do the following:

1. Develop a consistent set of questions that can be used for all candidates. Use of a special form can help ensure consistency (see Appendix F).

2. Have at least two selectors listen to the conversation.

3. Have the selectors take detailed notes based on the referees comments.

4. Inform the referee in advance as to whom the reference is about, and when the telephone call will be placed. This will give the previous employer a chance to consider the applicant's strengths and weaknesses.

The referee should know that more than one individual is listening to the telephone call, even if these others do not speak.

Written references have the advantage of providing a written record of any remarks made by the referee and provides greater control over what information is obtained. Its disadvantage is that there is less control over when the reference will be returned, the previous employer may be less forthright in making comments about the applicant, and there is no chance to follow-up and get an explanation unless a telephone reference is subsequently made.

When making the reference request, the previous employer should be informed of the name of the applicant and the position for which the applicant has applied. If possible, a description of the job to be filled should be included. Also, whenever possible, a copy of the applicant's signed agreement releasing referees from liability should be included. Among the information to be sought are:

- Confirmation of dates of employment.
- Confirmation of rate of pay at time of leaving.
- Confirmation of reason for leaving.
- Evaluation of attendance.
- Evaluation of quality and timeliness of work performed.
- Evaluation of ability to get along with others.
- Evaluation of candidate's work performance.
- Evaluation of candidate's ability to communicate orally or in writing.
- Evaluation of candidate's strengths and weaknesses.
- Indications of disciplinary actions in the last two years and reasons for disciplinary actions if any.
- Eligibility for rehire.
- Any other characteristics that are related to important functions of the job.

The form should also include space for the applicant's name (printed), a place for the signature of the referee, date, how long the referee has known the applicant, and in what capacity.

Employers should be aware that the administration of the reference process must be scrupulously fair. At whatever point reference checks are made, *all* candidates who have made it to that point should be subject to the reference procedure. If possible, the same number of reference checks per candidate should also be made. Although it is the responsibility of the employer to try to gather pertinent job-related information concerning the prospective employee, many employers, because of fear of liability, have decided only to give job title and dates of employment for job references. There is little that the prospective employer can do about this. Nonetheless, given the rather large percentage of applicants who falsify information on their applications, even this amount of verification may prove valuable.

Employers should also consider letters to educational institutions verifying the conferring of degrees. Stories of individuals who have claimed to have graduated from prestigious institutions are common in the business literature. Nothing is actually known about such distortions among library employees, but it would behoove the employer to make such a check at some point in the hiring process.

STEP 17: EVALUATE THE CANDIDATES

Once the interviews and reference checks have been made, it is time to select the best candidate. The hiring decision should be based on all the relevant information that has been gathered, not just the interview. Sometimes, the interview is seen as a contest in which the winner of the interview gets the "prize," i.e., the job. But this is not correct. The interview is but one important part of the information gathering process. Information from other sources such as the application form, resume, references, and examples of work performed in previous jobs also form a base on which to make the hiring decision.

On some occasions, the selection is easy: one candidate stands out above all the rest. However, even in this situation, the decision-making process should follow the same systematic course. First, a meeting of selectors should be convened. All selectors should be present. The complete files on each of the candidates should be available for review and discussion. Each selector should have a summary of each candidate's strengths and weaknesses including assessments of the candidates' knowledge, skill, and ability to perform the job. The job description should be reviewed. Each candidate should be discussed, not just the best candidate(s). When the number of qualified candidates has been narrowed to the two or three best qualified ones, the selectors, when relevant, should consider the affirmative action policy of the library to determine if the hire of any of the candidates would help meet the affirmative action goals of the institution. After this has been accomplished, the selectors must make a final decision. The overriding criteria is which candidate is the best one for the job.

One issue that arises in the selection decision-making process is whether a candidate's future potential in the organization should be considered. Although such a consideration is not itself illogical, the employer should be aware that the EEOC has determined that this issue should be considered only "if job progression structures are so established that employees will probably, within a reasonable period of time and in a majority of cases, progress to a higher level."[15] A reasonable period of time is considered about five years. What this means is that such a consideration is appropriate only if the employer can show that most of the employees hired into the position are promoted to the higher level position within five years. For example, considering the management skills of a librarian being hired for an entry-level position which requires no management responsibilities would be appropriate only if most entry-level librarians were promoted to management positions within a five-year period. This is unlikely in many libraries.

A second issue, which is especially important in a field like librarianship because it is numerically dominated by women, is to make sure that female candidates are given proper credit for their previous work experience. As noted before, there is some reason to believe that the successful performance of women is more often attributed to luck or ease of the task, rather than to ability and effort. Selectors must be scrupulous in evaluating fairly the performance of each candidate regardless of gender. Selectors must be careful that they do not undervalue successful women candidates or overvalue successful male ones.

A final criteria to be evaluated is called *applicant fit*. This is discussed in more detail in the section on hiring a library director. Suffice it to say here that once the candidates are determined to be at least minimally qualified for the job, there arises the question of how the individual will integrate into the specific work surroundings. This includes how they will respond to the organizational culture of the library, to the supervisory style of its managers, and how the individual will relate to peers and subordinates. There is a temptation to use "fit" as a final determiner among candidates. This could be a dangerous approach in that it is a highly subjective criterion, and one should be cautious about using such a criterion for this purpose. Rather, it might be better to employ it as a criterion to exclude individuals who *clearly* would not fit because of dispositional or other traits. In other words, unless a bad fit is determined, then the candidates should be evaluated on their other credentials.

When a final candidate has been selected, a list of job-related reasons for the selection should be prepared by the committee. This list forms the basis for documenting the hire in case there is a challenge. The selection and the reasons for it should be reviewed by an upper-level administrator or individual in charge of personnel before finalizing the decision to ensure compliance with all employment laws and regulations. If there is time, it might also be best to delay contacting the candidate for a period of 12-24 hours for further reflection. This allows the selectors time to "reconsider" should they experience subsequent misgivings. This waiting period, however, has the one disadvantage that the candidate may accept another position.

STEP 18: MAKE THE JOB OFFER

One of the most pleasant aspects of the hiring process is the chance to make the job offer to the successful candidate. This is usually done by telephone (or if it is an internal candidate it may be done in person). It is essential that the job offer be carefully controlled to ensure that only correct information is provided to the new employee. For this reason, it is best that one person be in charge of making the formal job offer. During the job offer specific information should be provided including date and time of first day of employment, pay, the supervisor's name and department, where to report for work, and if the employee is on a special status, such as a "probationary" status. If the hire has certain conditions, such as being dependent on the passing of a physical examination, this should be noted as well. All of this information should be confirmed in a follow-up letter (see Appendix G). It is vital that the individual making the offer, as well as all individuals who have supervisory or administrative authority of the new employee, make no statements that would imply contractual obligations beyond those formally provided by the employer. Such statement could be construed as "implied contracts" which could unduly obligate the employer and increase legal liabilities.

From time to time, candidates will request time to think about accepting the job. The decision to permit a candidate such time is up to the employer and would depend on how urgent the need is to fill the position. Generally, at least 24 hours should be allowed, and three to five days to consider a job offer is not unreasonable.

There is always the possibility that the first choice of the employer refuses the job offer. The reason for the refusal may affect the employer's subsequent actions. For example, if the issue is one of inadequate salary or benefits, and the employer has some flexibility in this area, then the employer may wish to continue negotiations, especially if the candidate is a strong one. In many cases, however, the candidate's rejection of the position is final, or the employer has only a few options. First, the employer can make another choice from the group of candidates who were interviewed. The advantage of this approach is that there are no additional hiring costs. A "second choice" can turn out to be quite successful, but the employer should only select that individual if there is confidence that he or she can perform well in the job. It is a poor idea to select the "second choice" just because repeating the hiring process is time consuming and requires additional money. Hiring the wrong person for the job is much more expensive. A second alternative is to go back to the pool of uninterviewed candidates to determine if there are any individuals who might be interviewed. It is possible that the skills or abilities of a candidate have been overlooked. This is less likely, however, if the hiring process has been systematically and carefully conducted. The advantage to this approach is that it is less time consuming and expensive than re-opening the hiring process, but it severely limits the pool of potential candidates. A third option is to leave the position vacant and to re-open the hiring process. From a short-term perspective, this is the most expensive choice, but there are many instances in which re-advertising a position produces new and well-qualified candidates. Some potential candidates may not have been ready for a job move when the first job announcement appeared.

If the employer chooses to re-open the hiring process, all previous candidates should be informed in writing. In addition, if re-opening the position was due to a candidate's rejection of the position, the employer should consider carefully the reason for the rejection, especially if it is based on factors in the control of the employer. The employer may want to make adjustments (e.g., salary, benefits, working conditions) before advertising the position again.

STEP 19: INFORM THE UNSUCCESSFUL CANDIDATES

For every successful candidate there are usually several unsuccessful ones and these individuals need to be informed promptly and in a business-like fashion that they were not selected for the position. This is usually done by letter. The letter should be prepared on good business stationary and sent first class to the candidate. It should be personally addressed rather than have a generic greeting. The letter should be short and to the point. It should indicate that another individual was selected for the position, but that the library appreciated the time taken by the candidate to participate in the hiring process. The letter should also indicate if the application will remain active in the library's files and for how long. In many cases it would not be inappropriate to wish the candidates good fortune in their search for future positions. It is not advisable to go into detail concerning the qualifications of the successful candidate or the inadequacies of the unsuccessful one. This would only encourage debate.

STEP 20: COMPLETE NECESSARY PAPER WORK

Any hiring process generates a significant amount of paper. This material needs to be organized, stored, and controlled. Most of the material consists of official forms such as applications, letters of reference, correspondence with applicants, applicant flow log, and formal reasons for selection. This material should be maintained in a separate file and stored in the director's or administrative offices. Personal notes of the selectors can be maintained in this file or stored in the selector's own files, but they should not be discarded. The length of time that such material should be retained may vary and legal advice should be obtained, but it would not be unwise to keep such material for five to seven years. Remember that such notes can play an important role if the hire is subsequently challenged.

There is a variety of paperwork which is maintained for the successful candidate. These include a copy of the letter of job offer, the application form, resume, and correspondence. In addition, new records are necessary including federal and state income tax withholding forms, insurance forms, and the I-9 form. All of this material is stored in the employee's new personnel file.

STEP 21: MONITOR THE HIRING PROCESS

For many hires it is useful simply to review the process with the selectors to determine if deficiencies exist and if more effective ways could have been employed to identify and hire qualified candidates. More importantly, a summary of applications and hiring decisions should be analyzed at the end of each year to determine if a disproportionate number of individuals from protected classes were screened out. If so, then the library would need to analyze the reasons for this result and to take corrective action if necessary (see Chapter 2).

HIRING THE LIBRARY DIRECTOR

The most important position in a library is that of the director. The director is critical to the activities of the organization, for setting the organizational tone, for maintaining and promoting an organizational culture, and for directing the activities of the organization toward specific goals. This means that considerable fiscal resources should be devoted to securing the best possible applicant. Attempting to save money when hiring a library director can lead to far more expensive consequences in the future.

The hiring of the director, especially for public libraries, is usually vested in the Board of Trustees. The director is responsible for carrying out the policies and plans established by the Board. For this reason, the Board must be able to delineate clearly their expectations and the direction in which they desire the director to take them.

For the most part, the steps that are taken as part of the general hiring process noted above can also be followed with this position. However, because of the special character of this position some additional considerations should be noted.

In preparation for hiring a director, the Board should be able to provide the following:

1. *A clearly written statement of the library's purpose and function in the community.* Actually, hiring a director provides a wonderful opportunity for the Board to re-evaluate the direction and function of the library. By dealing with this issue before the hiring process begins, the Board will have a clear and fresh understanding of where they want to go and what type of person they need to accomplish their goals.

2. *An accurate, up-to-date description of the community.* The Board should gather accurate data on the community's demographic, economic and cultural features.[16] This helps define the service emphases of the library and identifies any new directions for library. Gathering such information may well highlight important questions that should be asked of prospective candidates in the interview, and may also be used to provide background to the candidate as needed.

3. *A clearly written job description describing the functions and accountabilities of the position.* The position of director is complex and it is incumbent on the Board to provide a candidate with a clear idea of the Board members' expectations. By having a current job description, the interviewers can develop their questions to reflect the actual needs of the job. The Board must keep in mind that directorial positions are fundamentally administrative in nature and this means that although the possession of library skills may be necessary,

they are not sufficient to be a good director. The Board must also look for management skills such as planning, budgeting, personnel administration, political acumen, communications, and public relations.

4. *A sample of a basic contract which would indicate the terms and conditions of employment.* It is probably a good idea to have a separate written contract when hiring the library director, prepared by legal counsel. Such a contract would include the terms and conditions of employment including duration of the contract, conditions under which the contract may be terminated by either party, salary, benefits such as vacation, sick time, and retirement.

The recruitment strategy for library directors should be as broad as possible. Even for smaller libraries, if possible, recruitment should be national. Of course, the scope of the recruitment may depend on the time allotted and fiscal resources available. The sources for recruitment should include library publications, but may also include non-library ones such as *The Chronicle of Higher Education.*

The individuals who conduct the interviews usually consist of Board members in one of two arrangements: either a selected personnel committee appointed from among the Board members is created, or the entire Board itself screens candidates. An alternative approach might be to hire a consultant to screen the initial applicants and to refer to the Board only those applicants that pass the initial screening. This requires that the consultant have a very clear idea as to what the Board desires in terms of the knowledge, skills, and abilities of the prospective candidates.

There is no doubt that the knowledge, skills and abilities of the candidates, should, like any other position, play a major role in making the selection decision. Nonetheless, it is also vitally important, especially on this level that there is a fit between the Board members and the director. The concept of fit does not necessarily imply that the Board members and the director will agree on all matters, but the Board must be able to work cooperatively and effectively with its director. Unfortunately, the concept of "fit" is not a clear one and it is essential that the Board members have some specific idea as to what constitutes fit within the context of their specific organization. Fit might mean, for example, ability to communicate effectively and in a non-combative fashion; or it may mean possessing a consultative rather than authoritative personal and leadership style. It is crucial that the Board be honest with itself as to what it desires in the person to be hired, only then can an honest fit be determined. There are other dangers to the concept of fit as well. It is, for example, very easy to impose stereotypes when trying to assess this factor because it is so subjective; interviewers must be scrupulous that prejudices are not allow to creep in, for instance, that a woman would not fit as a library director. Similarly, fit should not be confused with "lack of initiative or creativity." An individual who fits in this sense, that is, who never rocks the boat may stimulate no changes, even those that are needed.[17]

REFERENCES

1. Richard D. Arvey and James E. Campion. "The Employment Interview: A Summary and Review of Recent Research," *Personnel Psychology* 35 (1982): 287, 293.

2. Ibid., p. 288.

3. Ibid., p. 293.

4. Ibid., p. 287.

5. Ibid., p. 298-300.

6. Richard Rubin, *Human Resource Management in Libraries*. New York: Neal Schuman, 1990, p. 55-56.

7. Eder, Robert W., K. Michele Kacmar, and Gerald R. Ferris. "Employment Interview Research: History and Synthesis," in *The Employment Interview: Theory, Research, and Practice*, edited by Robert W. Eder and Gerald R. Ferris, Newbury Park: Sage, 1989, p. 18.

8. Ronan, "Individual and Situation Variables Relating to Job Satisfaction," *Journal of Applied Psychology Monograph* 54 (February 1970): 28.

9. Arvey and Campion, p. 308-310.

10. Ibid., p. 281-322.

11. See for example, Kay Deaux and Tim Emswiller, "Explanations of Successful Performance on Sex-Linked Tasks: What is Skill for the Male is Luck for the Female," *Journal of Personality and Social Psychology* 29 (January 1974): 80-85; and Madeline E. Heilman and Richard A. Guzzo, "The Perceived Cause of Work Success as a Mediator of Sex Discrimination in Organizations," *Organizational Behavior and Human Performance* 21 (1978): 346-357.

12. John F. Binning, Mel A. Goldstein, Mario F. Garcia and Julie H. Scattaregia, "Effects of Preinterview Impressions on Questioning Strategies in Same- and

Opposite-Sex Employment Interviews," *Journal of Applied Psychology* 73 (February 1988): 34.

13. Arvey and Campion, p. 284-286.

14. Schippmann, Jeffrey S., Erich P. Prien, and Jerome A. Katz. "Reliability and Validity of In-Basket Performance Measures," *Personnel Psychology* 43 (1990): 837-59.

15. Part 1607, Uniform Guidelines on Employee Selection Procedures (1978), 1607.5(I).

16. For a good general discussion of this aspect of hiring see *Securing A New Library Director*. Chicago: ALA, ALTA, 1985.

17. For a detailed research-based discussion of applicant fit see Sara Rynes and Barry Gerhart, "Interviewer Assessments of Applicant "Fit": An Exploratory Investigation," *Personnel Psychology 43 (1990): 13-35.*

6 ORIENTATION AND TRAINING

The hiring process does not end until the new employee is comfortably situated in her new job. It is regrettable when an employer spends a great deal of time and money on the hiring process and then throws a new employee into a work situation with little guidance and support. An employee's commitment to the job can be extremely high before coming to work. After all, in most cases, the new employee knows only the good things about the organization; all or most of his contacts have been positive, and the employer has paid the new employee the compliment of selecting him as the candidate. At this stage the employee is excited to come to work and *wants* to like the organization. After all, the candidate has also chosen the employer, and it is a reflection of the candidate's own judgment. An unwise choice reflects badly on the candidate as well as the organization.

This psychological condition of excitement and high commitment makes it a perfect time to orient and train employees, because they will usually be highly motivated to learn the job. The employer should beware, however, that this condition also places the employer at considerable risk. While the commitment of an employee is high during this period, it is also very fragile. That is, the commitment is based on little or no real experience in the workplace. As a result, early experiences that are negative can substantially alter this commitment and turn excitement to frustration and discontent. If the employer makes errors in this early stage, the damage can lead to poor morale, poor performance and high employee turnover.

If an employer has no formal orientation system, at the very least, all employees should receive a written copy of major policies and practices of the library. This might be found in an employee handbook. In addition, the employer should provide what is called a *realistic job preview*. Put simply, the employer should provide an accurate, realistic assessment of the conditions that the employee will confront on the job, and on the opportunities of the job. Part of this information should have already been provided during the job interview. Realism is essential. New employees, because of their excitement, may have unrealistic expectations of the job and the employer. Although the employer should not try to dampen this excitement, disappointed expectations are an especially damaging occurrence to employee satisfaction. Creating unrealistic expectations are, consequently, a self-defeating activity. When the orientation and training is completed, the employee should feel comfortable and welcome in her new workplace, excited about coming to work, and clear on the tasks that she is expected to perform.

ORIENTATION

Orientation is distinguished from training in that it provides employees with a much broader perspective as to how they fit into the organization as a whole. Although it may include the training of the employee, it includes much more information and has a different purpose. It is a critical function, because it provides a great opportunity to welcome the employee into the organization and to have him or her feel "at-home." For this reason, careful preparation must be paid not only to the specific information that is conveyed but also to the effect of the orientiation on the attitudes of the new employee. Following orientation, it is hoped that the employee will have a positive attitude, have a feeling of belonging, and retain his or her excitement for working.

The employee may receive orientation from one individual or from a combination of people and informational sources. She may be oriented by the director or personnel officer, by immediate supervisors, or by fellow staff. What is essential is that responsibility for various aspects of the orientation is clearly delegated to particular individuals. The orientation program should be systematic and standardized, so that all employees receive the same basic information. To assume that the overall orientation is thorough, it is best if the employer follows an orientation checklist which is maintained in the administrative offices (see Appendix H).

A systematic orientation process deals with many issues and covers many important topics. For this reason, it should not be assumed that it will all be accomplished in one day. Among the many topics that are covered are the following:

THE PHILOSOPHY OF THE ORGANIZATION

A vital, but often overlooked area of orientation is a discussion of the values and goals of the organization. Among the factors that produce commitment among employees is the employee's belief that meaningful work is being performed and that others rely on the work of the employee. Libraries have it easy in this regard, because there are many valued and important functions that libraries perform. Nonetheless, the employer should not assume that each new employee understands this. The employee's supervisor or an appropriate administrator should discuss explicitly the philosophy of the library and its service. The goals of the library should be reviewed and the importance of library work should be emphasized. The value that the library places on each employee should be noted, including the fact that library work is interdependent: that no job is unimportant and that many other jobs rely on the proper performance of individual jobs. If the goals, mission, or philosophy of library service have been published, then the appropriate documents should be given to the employee.

Important organizational policies and practices: Any organization has a set of established policies, practices, and customs. It is normal for new employees to be especially sensitive about making mistakes so it is a good idea to review the major policies and practices of the library and to discuss how the library is organized. Once the employee has been hired, it is useful to send any written materials on the organizational rules and practices to the employee before she comes to work. Subsequently, the director or an administrator should be responsible for reviewing such material with the new employee so that the substance and interpretation of institutional policies is consistently expressed. Because such discussion will often take place in an administrative office, this may also be a convenient time to complete the necessary paperwork for employment including tax-withholding forms and forms for hospitalization and the retirement system. Among the areas to be covered when discussing policies and practices are the following:

1. The terms and conditions of employment including job status (i.e., probationary, temporary, etc.) and rate of current pay.
2. How the wage system is administered in terms of raises, cost of living and merit increases.
3. Benefits available including sick leave, vacation time, hospitalization and dental benefits and other prominent benefits. Discussion should also include the procedure for using sick leave (e.g., whom to report to if ill) and scheduling vacations.

4. How individuals are paid (completing time cards, how often, where, and from whom checks are received).

5. Grievance and employment discrimination complaint procedures including sexual harassment guidelines.

6. Philosophy and procedures established to deal with unsatisfactory performance.

7. Important organizational rules such as need for prompt attendance, employee attitude and conduct, appearance, and rules regarding breaks and meals.

8. Review of staff facilities, discussion of the physical organization of the library.

Review of the job description: The new employee should have a clear idea of the tasks of the job. A full discussion of the job should include not only the tasks to be performed, but just as important if not more so, the employee should see how the job fits into the organization as a whole. This involves a discussion of the major accountabilities of the job. Emphasis should be placed on the goals of the job—what is to be accomplished by the job and why those goals are important to the organization as a whole. Again, job interdependence should be emphasized by specifically indicating which departments or positions rely on the employee to perform well, and the importance of the job in regard to service to library patrons.

Review of performance standards: An employee should not only know what she is to do, but also what level of performance is considered acceptable or superior. This is not always easy when dealing with library positions. Nonetheless, the employee should be able to review whatever standards of performance have been established and have a chance to see the forms used for rating employee performance. This is also a good opportunity to emphasize the performance culture of the organization. Best performance is obtained when supervisors and the organization set clear, difficult, and challenging goals. By communicating to the employee that the organization sets high expectations for performance, the appropriate climate for high productivity is established. (Of course, the organization must be able to provide competent supervision and resources or the employee's expectations will be disappointed, leading to job dissatisfaction, poor morale, and employee turnover.)

Opportunities for development: A library's attitude toward its employees is, in part, reflected in the resources it devotes toward their improvement. The employer should indicate in what situations the employee may receive financial and other assistance when seeking further education and training through formal instruction, workshops, or attendance at professional conferences.

Opportunities for advancement: Many employees perceive their entry position as just the beginning of a career and movement upward in the organization is important to them. This is natural in that upward movement is considered to increase both status and pay. The employer should be realistic concerning the future opportunities within the organization. A discussion of how promotions are received, and what additional education and training is needed for certain jobs is appropriate. The employer must be very careful, however, not to make promises that would lead the employee to believe that promotion is to be expected, or that internal candidates are preferred over external ones (unless such is the policy of the library).

Review of physical facility and staff introductions: A useful part of orientation involves orienting the employee to his or her physical surroundings. This "tour" is often conducted by the immediate supervisor. Of course, the employee should be able to see the specific work area and be introduced to the staff members with whom she will be working. As far as possible, the employee should then be given a tour of the larger facility indicating key departments with whom the employee will be making contact and introducing additional staff members. Areas such as lunch rooms, restrooms, and administrativee offices should be visited. In addition, when appropriate, rules regarding access to security areas should be noted.

Closing the orientation: At the end of the orientation process, the individual in charge of orientation should have a meeting with the new employee, make sure that all orientation procedures have been followed, have the employee sign the orientation checklist (see Appendix H), and answer any questions that the employee may have about her employment. (The signed checklist should be placed in the employee's personnel file.) This is also a good opportunity to express confidence in the candidate that they will be a productive member of the staff.

TRAINING

Training is usually considered the provision of information to employees to assist employees in the performance of their specific jobs. This is sometimes referred to as "instrumental" information. Some of this information is not wholly distinct from orientation in that discussions of such things as job descriptions and standards of performance will coincide or be coordinated between those who orient employees and those who train them. Because most jobs involve direct supervision, the individual responsible for training is usually the immediate supervisor, although other co-workers may and often do become involved.

Failure to train properly can have devastating consequences. Creth identifies five consequences of poor training: poor performance, low productivity, need for increased supervision, higher employee turnover, and discipline and motivation problems in the workplace.[1] As with orientation, the organization sends a message to the employee by the quality of training provided. An institution that is sloppy in its training tells the employee that the institution is unprofessional and uncaring. This is a poor impression and can become an unfortunate source of negative feelings in the new employee.

The purpose of training the new employee is twofold: first, to help make the employee more comfortable by familiarizing the employee with the job and the employees with whom the employee will work. This will give the employee the necessary information and time to master the job. Second, the training period gives the supervisor an opportunity to make an assessment of the employee's abilities and skills and to determine if the employee is appropriately matched to the position. Although a training program may be standardized, it is important to realize that each employee is different and will respond to training in relation to individual motivation, intelligence, personality, willingness to work hard, and manual dexterity. Despite these differences, however, the employer can be of great help by creating a supportive context in which training occurs.

PREREQUISITES TO GOOD TRAINING

Good training requires good preparation. Among the factors to be considered are the following:

The availability of good trainers: Before providing training, consider which staff members would make superior trainers. Although the immediate supervisor is traditionally thought of as the individual who is responsible for the training of the employee, this does not necessarily mean that the immediate supervisor actually *does* all or most of the training. If there are co-workers who have the requisite characteristics of a good trainer then they should be considered as important players in this process. Good trainers generally have at least three characteristics:

1. *They are good role models*—employees will model their behavior based on those who train them, especially if the trainer is perceived as having good skills.[2] If a new employee is trained by an individual whose skills and knowledge are inadequate or whose behavior is unprofessional and exhibits poor work attitudes, then a serious problem may result in the new employee. Attitudes set early in the job experience may be costly and difficult to overcome. Trainers must be made aware of the serious responsibility they have to serve as excellent models for their new co-workers.

2. *Trainers must be committed to the training process*—if a trainer sends a message by her attitude and actions that the training is unimportant or an imposition on her time, the employee is not likely to absorb the necessary information and job values.

3. *Trainers must have strong communication skills*—it is useless to place an individual in a training capacity who has difficulty with expression or demonstrating necessary job techniques. Such an individual will only frustrate the new worker and be an obstacle to good performance. Good trainers must be able to write and speak well, have knowledge of good teaching techniques, and be responsive and supportive to the learner. They have to be perceived by the learner as a good coach, as an individual who provides positive feedback. The trainer must inspire self-confidence in the employee, because an employee who believes that she can master the job is much more likely to be successful.

Having a clear understanding of the training structure and schedule: Good training requires a pre-existing structure that includes identification and training of trainers, creation of written and/or audiovisual materials to assist in training, identification of the essential content to be mastered, identification of the techniques to be applied and a schedule for application, and identification of techniques for measurement and evaluation of the training process.

Having a clear understanding of the job to be performed: Good training cannot proceed unless there is a clear understanding of the job. Current job descriptions, prior discussion with the previous staff members who performed the job, and discussions with the immediate supervisor and co-workers will assist in this understanding.

Having appropriate materials: Before providing training, it is usually necessary to prepare written and/or audio-visual materials which would assist in the training process (see "Types of Materials"). Employers should take time to prepare these materials in a professional manner for the same reasons it is important to use quality trainers. The success of the training exercise may well depend on the way information is presented as much as what information is provided.

Having the time and resources to train well: Training often receives short shrift in organizations often because they feel there is insufficient time. But well-trained employees save time because they make fewer mistakes and require less supervision. The organization must make sure that plenty of time is given to the trainer to provide the necessary information and to the trainee to practice and review what needs to be learned. This means that the necessary equipment and physical resources must also be available in a timely fashion.

Having a means for measurement and evaluation of training: Any training process requires that the process be evaluated. Typical types of measurement tools are paper and pencil tests, demonstrations of the tasks to be performed, or on-the-job observation. Of primary importance is to determine if *training transfer* has taken place, that is, can the employee take what is learned in the training setting and actually apply it in the work setting? Remember that training is an interactive process and that different training techniques may be employed depending on the characteristics of the employee and trainer.

In most cases, of course, the measurement of training effectiveness will be based on the close supervision of the employee by the supervisor during a probationary period. During this period, the supervisor's job is not only to observe employee performance, but to invite the employee to ask questions whenever necessary, and to provide feedback to the employee as problems or issues arise. In addition, the supervisor should communicate with co-workers to obtain additional information regarding the new employee's performance. Regular, sit-down sessions with the employee during this period is also useful when the various aspects of the job are reviewed and problems discussed.

TYPES OF TRAINING

There are many types of training that can be provided to new employees. The employer should consider many different training techniques depending on the job to be performed. This should include combinations of training techniques when appropriate.

On-the-job Training

The most common type is on-the-job training, whereby the employee is placed in position and supervised. The job may have many components, and a new employee may be asked to perform only part of the job at the beginning and as the employee increases in experience, the remaining portions of the job are performed. On-the-job training has the distinct advantage that the actual tasks are being performed, there is no need to wonder if the information provided will transfer to the job because it is the job. The primary disadvantage is that this type of training, in the absence of additional training techniques, is not systematic. The training consists of whatever experience the individual has at the time. These experiences may or may not be typical of the experiences on the job over a longer period of time. Hence, certain information may not be learned because the relevant situation did not arise.

Job Rotation

Job rotation allows the employee to perform in the jobs of other employees for a short time to learn about these jobs. Often these jobs are directly related to the employee's new position. New library employees may, for example, be moved from one library department to another for specified periods of time. The purpose of such rotation is to give an employee a broader perspective of the job and the organization. By providing the new employee with a view of the interdependence of the position, there is increased chance the employee will understand how important her position is and the greater the chance the new employee will consider her job meaningful. This, in turn, increases, job commitment.

Classroom or Workshop Instruction

Although less common than on-the-job training, some employers train employees through classroom or workshop instruction. Generally, new employees are more likely to be exposed to workshops, although classroom experience may subsequently occur as a form of staff development or preparation for professional work. Common workshops for new employees might include workshops on basic reference sources and reference interviewing for non-degree staff working with the public, or a workshop on dealing with problem employees. New supervisors might receive training workshops on supervision, performance evaluation, or job interviewing. This type of training has the advantage of being able to train a comparatively large number of individuals at one time. In addition, because one or two people conduct the workshop for all participants, the quality and content of the workshop can be controlled. One drawback to this type of training is that it is seldom done by the immediate supervisor. This means that the training tends to be more general and specific information about policies and practices on the job may be unavailable.

Role Playing

Because on-the-job training is relatively uncontrolled in terms of the experiences during the training period, role playing can serve as a valuable supplement. Role playing allows the participants to imitate real life situations by acting them out. This allows the employer to control the situation so that certain important experiences can be simulated to permit the new employee to practice. For example, when training reference personnel, one staff member may play the role of an unruly patron while the new employee plays the role of the reference librarian. Role playing is a form of practice and in order for it to be most effective, the situations simulated should conform as closely as possible to real life situations in the workplace.

FACTORS RELATED TO THE EFFECTIVENESS OF TRAINING

Aside from the trainer, there are several factors that determine whether the training itself will be effective. These factors include: 1. the characteristics of the trainee: ability, personality, and motivation, 2. how the training is designed: the content, sequence, and teaching principles used, and 3. the work environment: the support of trainers and administrators and the opportunity to use training.[3]

Characteristics of the trainee

Three aspects should be especially considered when determining whether the trainee is ready for training: expectations, locus of control, and motivation.

First, the employee's expectations should be considered. An employee who does not believe that the desired rewards will follow from training is unlikely to absorb the necessary information. Generally speaking, for new employees, their expectation is that the information will help them perform their jobs effectively. The training will be considered valuable if it does so and a source of frustration if it does not.

The second aspect involves a psychological condition known as "locus of control."[4] Locus of control deals with the extent to which an individual believes that she is personally in control of what happens to her. Persons with an "internal" locus of control feel that they are responsible for the events that happen to them; while those with an "external" locus of control believe that the events that happen to them are usually the result of luck, fate, or circumstances.[5] Employees with an internal locus of control are desired when it comes to training because such individuals are more likely to believe that the information that they absorb can help them bring the environment under control; those with an external locus are less likely to perceive that the information is valuable because they are powerless to control events.

The third aspect is the new employee's motivation. Employees who want to be trained are much better candidates for training transfer than those who do not. Training transfer occurs best when three motivational conditions are met: 1. employees believe that they had a choice in the training, 2. employees have a high level of job commitment, and 3. employees believe that they will be applying the training directly in their job.[6] In the second and third instances, the new employee is bound to share these beliefs and in the first instance it is unlikely that the employee would expect such training to be her own choice. In other words, the conditions for effective training should be considerable from a motivational perspective.

TRAINING DESIGN

Fundamentally, the training process is one of teaching and communication. There are two features that are essential in any well-designed training program. These are opportunity for feedback and opportunity to practice.

Opportunity for feedback: Employees need and deserve to know how they are performing. Trainers should pay special attention to both the timing of the feedback and its specificity. Corrections should be made immediately or as soon as is practically possible to ensure that the new employee does not practice errors. Of course, the trainer must be careful not to be too critical or overdo the feedback. The new employee should not be made to feel that she is under constant surveillance. In addition, the willingness of individuals to change their behavior is affected by the amount of criticism given. If the new employee feels that the amount of criticism is too great, she may respond by feeling frustrated, depressed, angry, stupid, and fearful. This fear may arise quite rationally from the fact that she may be on a temporary or probationary status. The employee may develop a poor attitude and low motivation, neither of which is usually productive for the employer. This highlights the need for trainers to offer compliments and encouragement whenever possible. It is human to want to continue performing tasks which result in positive rewards and to discontinue those that have negative effects. The trainer must not be stingy with compliments; in so far as they are appropriate they can create a good psychological foundation for the entire training process.

Opportunity for Practice: No training can be effective if the employee is not permitted an opportunity to demonstrate in practice what she has learned. When developing the conditions for practice, the following issues should be considered:[7]

1. *Active practice*: The employee should be given clear instruction and then allowed to practice what she has been taught. Generally the instruction-practice cycle

(sometimes called "cumulative rotation") should be repeated to allow for variation in the learning process until the entire task is learned.8 Preferably practice should be "real," that is, the actual activity is being performed. To the extent that this is impossible, the practice should be as close to the real task as possible. Giving an employee a test in which she regurgitates the information she received is not practice and is insufficient.

2. *Overlearning*: Employees must be allowed to practice repeatedly even after they have completed the tasks successfully. By allowing extended repetition, the knowledge becomes so deeply ingrained that performance of the task becomes automatic.

3. *Distributed practice*: The employee should be permitted to practice over a lengthy period of time rather than being permitted to practice at one time only. Allow practice sessions to be broken up with other types of work.

4. *Size of practice unit*: Many jobs require that the employee learn a variety of interrelated, smaller tasks. Generally, employees need to learn smaller tasks first which are subsequently combined. Of course, some tasks are less conducive to learning one thing at a time. For example, in training a reference librarian, it is difficult just to train them to answer the telephone; rather she needs to be trained to answer the telephone, use the card catalog, and answer the question all in combination. Clerical tasks on the other hand are more amenable to learning distinct tasks separately.

5. *Relevance*: The employee must perceive that the training is directly related to her work, and that the information is valuable. For new employees, this relationship may be obvious, because the training should relate directly to the tasks of her new job. Nonetheless, managers should be aware that employees undergoing training need to see that the training is clearly associated with the work to be performed.

6. *Use of Examples*: Sometimes referred to as "stimulus variability," training programs need to be designed so that the instructional material includes many different

examples to get across the major points of the training. Research indicates that the use of a variety of examples when providing instruction is superior to one example used repeatedly.[9]

WORK ENVIRONMENT

As with any form of education, the learning environment plays a vital role. The climate which the employer wants to create should be supportive, open, and nonthreatening. A nonthreatening environment implies that the new employee feels at ease asking questions and making comments. In addition, it implies an understanding that making mistakes is a natural part of the process and is subject to gentle correction and encouragement. Obviously, the supervisor plays a critical role in this process. The supervisor must exhibit confidence that the employee will succeed, and assure the employee that help will be provided as needed.[10] If the new entrant fears punishment or humiliation for errors during the training period, or suspects that she will not get the help and cooperation needed, then she is not likely to learn well, or develop a positive work attitude.

TYPES OF MATERIALS

In developing materials for training, there are two different types: print and audiovisual. The use of such materials depends on the purpose of the training and the type of individuals to be trained.

1. Print materials

Some information is best imparted by giving the employee an opportunity to review written material. Some of this material may be instructions especially prepared for training purposes, or they may be pre-existing materials. Among the items most likely to be best transmitted in writing would be staff handbooks containing library policies, job descriptions, department procedure manuals, and examples of work to be performed. Providing training through written materials has the distinct advantage that employees can, within limits, pace themselves, reading and re-reading the material as needed. In addition, they can choose to learn the material in any order, rather than in an order imposed by the trainer.[11]

2. Audiovisual materials

Audiovisual materials are experiencing increased use in the training process. With the advent of the videocassette, video production and playback is much simpler and libraries can make their own training tapes. The flexibility of the VCR is tremendous. It can be used in a group setting or it can be sent home with an individual employee. Video training tools are, for example, very useful for demonstrating particular library practices, or for showing individuals how to deal with patrons or how to handle reference interviews. The employee can actually see the application of the technique. Similarly, videos can also be used for self-evaluation. For example, new reference librarians can be taped in actual or practice interviews. The tapes can subsequently be replayed for the employee and analyzed for strengths and weaknesses. In addition, because of the potential impact of visual images, videos can be used to instill a feeling of commitment to the library and its purpose. For new employees this can be particularly effective because they are generally eager to adopt the philosophy of the organization so that they can integrate easily into the work environment.

Videos, generally, are most effective when they are combined with other training techniques, including written materials, and a trainer or facilitator. The presence of trainers is especially important because unless a trainer is present, the trainee is unable to ask questions for clarification. A drawback to video is that it is more difficult to repeat parts of a film or tape, or to change the order of presentation.

MENTORING

Mentoring can be a very effective method to train new employees and use the skills of experienced employees beyond that of performing their regular work. Formal mentoring involves the assignment of a more senior individual to the new employee to assist the employee in his or her adjustment to the new organization and to promote the employee's success. The advantages to the protege are considerable:

1. Perhaps most important, mentors provide an effective role model for successful performance. Modelling behavior is one of the best ways to encourage similar behavior in the learner. When an employee perceives good organizational attitudes and values in a successful employee, this increases the chance that the behavior will be imitated.

2. Mentors give new employees a sense of security and self-confidence because they know there is an individual who can answer their questions and assist them when they have problems.

3. Mentors usually have many excellent contacts within the organization and can therefore provide opportunities to develop their careers.

4. Mentors can also help protect an individual by warning the employee about politically dangerous situations or about individuals who are destructive to the organization.

5. Mentors can be a source for recommendations and support when the new employee is considered for promotion.

The advantages of a mentoring program are not only for the protege. The mentor may also experience considerable benefits including confirmation that their knowledge and experience is valuable—giving the mentor an opportunity to meet new challenges for using knowledge.[12]

If a library decides to develop a mentoring program several factors should be kept in mind regarding both the mentor and the protege:

1. *Age*: Generally, the mentor should be older and possess considerable experience. However, the age gap should not be too great, perhaps eight to 15 years.[13]

2. *Success*: The mentor should be successful in the field. There is little productive use in assigning proteges to individuals who are not competent role models. The mentor should be an individual who has demonstrated or who has the capacity to demonstrate high performance.

3. *Gender*: Mentor and protege should be of the same sex if possible. This decreases the possibility of sexual relationships developing and diminishes the chance that stereotypes will be imposed in the relationship.

4. *Power*: The mentor should be highly placed in the organization and not threatened by the success of the protege.[14]

5. *Performance*: The protege should be an employee who has demonstrated high performance or the capacity of such performance. Noe suggests that the best proteges are those that believe that their success will depend on their own performance.[15]

A mentoring program is a dynamic one. As the protege matures, the relationship passes through at least four stages.[16]

1. Initiation stage: The initiation stage usually involves the first six to 12 months. This period is characterized by the protege's admiration and respect for the mentor. The relationship is characterized by support.

2. Cultivation stage: This stage occurs for approximately two to five years. The mentor provides the greatest benefit during this period as she helps develop the protege's career, sponsoring the employee for promotions, providing challenges on the job, and protecting the employee from those who might try to damage the protege's career.

3. Separation stage: This is a stage in which a new equilibrium is established. The protege begins to develop both a psychological, professional, and, in some cases, geographical independence. This can cause strains on the mentor as the dependency of the protege is significantly diminished. The mentor may even feel threatened by the increasing success of the protege. In rare cases, the mentor may begin to block the protege's promotional opportunities.

4. Redefinition stage: If the mentoring has been successful, this stage leads the mentor and protege to see each other as equals. The peer relationship that develops may take some time before both are comfortable. Often this leads to a strong friendship. In some cases,

the redefined relationship is not positive. The protege may feel estranged by the mentor and anger and hostility may result.

Although mentoring can be an extremely beneficial process, it is clear that there are several potential pitfalls as well. Among the areas the employer must monitor are the following:

1. Ensure that eligibility for mentoring programs is based on objective criteria. Because a disproportionate number of administrative and managerial positions are held by males, employers should be scrupulous about avoiding an "old boys' network" when offering opportunities for mentorships. In addition, opportunities for mentoring should not be based on pre-established friendships or family relationships.

2. Attempt to assign mentors to individuals with complementary personalities. Mentoring requires the development of close bonds and loyalties; individuals who are not compatible are likely to develop destructive relationships.

3. The responsibilities of the protege should be substantial. Mentors should not be permitted to use employees as errand runners, to fill in for vacant positions, or to perform busy-work. The purpose of mentoring is to develop and train the employee.

4. Mentors should be selected for their knowledge, managerial and interpersonal skills. Individuals who are inclined to punish, to be possessive, or to be dictatorial should be avoided.

5. Cross-gender mentorships, usually male mentors and female proteges, should be avoided if possible. As noted above, successful mentor relationships involve the development of emotional as well as professional bonds. The possibility that such relationships could lead to romantic entanglements or the perception of such entanglements could create serious problems. This is not to say that cross-gender mentorships should be prohibited; this may be a necessity in many libraries. Nonetheless, the employer should be aware of the special problems. If a male-female mentorship is involved, several

steps can be taken to diminish potential problems. First, the mentor should provide opportunities for other managers to observe the performance of and work with the protege. If the mentor subsequently recommends promotion for the protege, others will have observed the quality of the protege's performance themselves. This lessens the possibility that the mentor's recommendation was based on sexual rather than professional reasons. Second, discourage "after-hour," or extended, or unscheduled private meetings that provide fodder to inappropriate speculation on the part of others. Third, avoid pet expressions, names, or inside jokes signifying a more than professional relationship. Fourth, avoid touching, hugging, or other forms of intimacy with the protege. Although these actions may be perfectly innocent, it jeopardizes the perceived objectivity of the mentor and the abilities of the protege.[17]

Despite the pitfalls of mentoring, there is little doubt that it offers one of the best opportunities for employees to develop the necessary contacts and skills for career development. As such, library managers should seriously consider developing such programs or encouraging informal mentoring in their absence.

ADDITIONAL FACTORS THAT INCREASE SUCCESS FOR NEW EMPLOYEES

Training and orientation are just one part of the everyday responsibility of supervisors to encourage, reward, and correct employee performance. Good training is no substitute for continuous, quality supervision. Once formal orientation and training are concluded, the employer must continue to shape the workplace so that the motivation of the employee to work hard remains high. As noted earlier, there are a variety of factors that stimulate the desire in workers to remain with their organization. These factors are especially critical for the new employee who is vulnerable and particularly sensitive to his or her new work surroundings. Employers should therefore pay particular attention to these factors:

Make early job tasks interesting

An employee's first set of job assignments can have a significant effect on their job satisfaction and commitment. As a rule, individuals prefer to perform interesting tasks, tasks with responsibility and variety. These types of tasks should be provided from the very beginning. The library employee's early experience should involve the most interesting aspects of the job rather than the least interesting. It is an unfortunate habit of some employers that they assign routine work at the beginning to provide employees with "the basics" first to learn the job "from the ground up." Although routine activities are important, the employee should also be performing work that is not routine. By providing enriching work early in the employee's experience, the employer increases the chances that the employee will have high job satisfaction. Provide jobs that create a feeling in the worker that she is responsible for accomplishing the broader organizational goals.

New employees want to feel that they are part of the organization and make a contribution to it. This is sometimes referred to as felt responsibility. Because new employees often need to concentrate on performing their specific tasks well, they may not be conscious of their broader contribution to the whole. This can be exacerbated by the bureaucratic, departmental structures common in libraries that tend to separate organizational units. Supervisors must pay special attention to ensuring that new employees understand how important their work is to the greater organization.

Create opportunities for making contacts and friends

New employees often have no friends or acquaintances in the workplace when they begin working. It is crucial that new employees not feel alienated. Work groups should be made aware that cliques that tend to exclude new individuals reduce the chances that the new worker will remain. This is especially important for highly productive new workers; if they perceive that their success does not depend on the work of others, and that they are not appreciated by their co-workers, they are much more likely to leave. The organization should also attempt to involve the new worker as early as possible in larger organizational activities such as committees so that she becomes linked to the organization as a whole, not just to her department.

REFERENCES

1. Creth, Sheila D. *Effective On-The-Job Training*. Chicago: American Library Association, 1986:10.

2. Wexley, Kenneth N. and Gary P. Latham, *Developing and Training Human Resources in Organizations*. Dallas: Scott, Foresman, 1981:69.

3. Baldwin, Timothy T. and J. Kevin Ford, "Transfer of Training: A Review and Directions for Further Research," *Personnel Psychology* 41 (Spring 1988):63.

4. Rotter, J.B. *Social Learning and Clinical Psychology*. Englewood Cliffs, N.J.: Prentice-Hall, 1954.

5. Noe, Raymond A. "Trainees' Attributes and Attitudes: Neglected Influences on Training Effectiveness," *Academy of Management of Review* 11 (October 1986): 69.

6. Baldwin and Ford; p. 69.

7. The following material on practice was taken from Richard Rubin, *Human Resource Management in Libraries*. New York: Neal-Schuman, 1991.

8. Lyle M. Ehrenberg, "How to Ensure Better Transfer of Learning," *Training and Development Journal* (February 1983): 82.

9. Baldwin and Ford, p. 67.

10. Wexley and Latham, p. 69.

11. Rabin, Jack, Thomas Vocino, W. Barley Hildreth, and Gerald J. Miller, eds. *Handbook on Public Personnel Administration and Labor Relations*. New York: Marcel Deckker: 1983, p. 213.

12. Hunt, David Marshall and Carol Michael, "Mentoring: A Career Training and Development Tool," *Academy of Management Review* 8 (1983): 475.

13. Hunt and Michael, p. 479.

14. Hunt and Michael, pp. 480-482.

15. Raymond A. Noe, "An Investigation of the Determinants of Successful Assigned Mentoring Relationships," *Personnel Psychology* 41 (Autumn 1988):461.

16. Kathy E. Kram, "Phases of the Mentor Relationship," *Academy of Management Journal* 26 (1983): 608-625.

17. James G. Clawson and Kathy E. Kram, "Managing Cross-Gender Mentoring," *Business Horizons* 27 (May/June 1984): 29.

7 DEALING WITH THE ADA

There can be no doubt that the Americans with Disabilities Act (ADA) has an effect on the hiring process. Indeed, it was intended to do so. The ADA is a recognition that individuals with disabilities have been inappropriately screened out of the hiring process as well as other aspects of employment. The information provided in this section is based primarily on materials provided in the *Technical Assistance Manual from the Americans with Disabilities Act* provided by the Equal Employment Opportunity Commission.[1] (Page references in parenthesis refer to this document.)

For all intents and purposes, all libraries are governed by the ADA because it covers private employers, state, and local governments. Currently it covers employers with 25 or more employees; by July 1994 it will cover all employers with 15 or more employees. This includes part-time employees working 20 or more calendar weeks in the current or previous year. The ADA protects against discrimination in a wide variety of employment practices. In terms of the hiring process, the law covers such processes as applications, testing, hiring, job assignments, medical examinations, compensation, and benefits.

The ADA protects "qualified individuals with disabilities" from discrimination. According to the law, a person who has a disability is one who:

1. Has a physical or mental impairment that substantially limits one of more of his or her major life activities.

2. Has a record of such an impairment.

3. Is regarded as having such an impairment.

In addition, the law covers individuals who are perceived as having a relationship or association to an individual with a disability. For example, if an applicant's son or spouse is disabled, the applicant may claim discrimination if the disability of the spouse or son is taken into account in the hiring process.

The concept of a disability is broadly construed under the law. A "physical impairment" is:

> . . . any physiological disorder, or condition, cosmetic disfigurement, or anatomical loss affecting one or more of the following body systems: neurological, musculoskeletal, special sense organs, respiratory (including speech organs), cardiovascular, reproductive, digestive, genito-urinary, hemic and lymphatic, skin, and endocrine (p. II-2).

The definition of a "mental impairment" is equally broad:

> . . . any mental or psychological disorder, such as mental retardation, organic brain syndrome, emotional or mental illness, and specific learning disabilities (p. II-2).

There are obviously many illnesses and impairments that clearly fit under these definitions. There are, additionally, other conditions that may qualify depending on the situation. For example, stress might or might not be considered an impairment according to the EEOC depending on whether the stress is simply general due to the pressure of life, or whether the individual is diagnosed as having a "stress disorder" (II-3). In addition, a contagious disease like tuberculosis might be considered a disability, but the employer is not required to hire an individual who poses a direct threat to the health and safety of others.

Before any of these conditions qualify as a disability, they must be significant enough to "substantially limit the major life activities" of the employee. These activities are also broadly construed and include walking, seeing, speaking, hearing, breathing, learning, performing manual tasks, caring for oneself, and working. The substantiality of the limitation is measured by the extent, duration, and impact of the impairment. If an impairment is short-lived and has little impact on the employee's functioning, it is much less likely to be considered as a disability. Examples of impairments that would generally not be considered disabilities would be broken limbs, colds, flu, and appendicitis. (Exceptions could be made however if the duration of the problem extends beyond the normal recovery period.) If, however, even insubstantial impairments are perceived by the future employer as substantial, then the applicant is protected by the law. For example, if the future employer knows that a prospective employee has high blood pressure or epilepsy and considers this as a factor in the hiring process, discrimination could easily be involved especially if the condition is under medical control.

Given the broadness of the definitions, there are literally millions of Americans who qualified as disabled under the law. The exclusions are few, but among them are individuals who use drugs illegally (although those who are under rehabilitation *are* covered) and individuals who are homosexual or bisexual. Sexual orientation is not, in and of itself, considered to be a disability. It should be noted that alcoholics are not considered to be illegal drug users and therefore generally covered by the ADA. However, if the alcoholic's performance is poor, he or she may be disciplined in the same manner as any other employee.

WHAT ARE THE TYPES OF ACTIONS THAT ARE CONSIDERED DISCRIMINATORY?

There are a variety of actions which are considered discriminatory under the ADA. Among them are the following (I-4):

> Limiting, segregating, or classifying a job applicant or employee in a way that adversely affects employment opportunities for the applicant or employee because of his or her disability.

> Denying employment opportunities to a qualified individual because she or he has a relationship or association with a person with a disability.

> Refusing to make reasonable accommodation to the known physical or mental limitations of a qualified applicant or employee with a disability unless the accommodation would pose an undue hardship on the business.

> Using qualification standards, employment tests, or other selection criteria that screen out or tend to screen out an individual with a disability unless they are job related and necessary for the business.

In regard to the hiring process, the law specifically protects such employment practices as (I-4):

- Recruitment, advertising, and job application practices
- Hiring and rehiring
- Rates of pay or any other form of compensation
- Job assignment, classification, position descriptions
- Fringe benefits
- Selection and financial support for training (VII-2)

HOW DO YOU KNOW IF A PERSON IS QUALIFIED?

A person with a disability is considered "qualified" if he or she:

> satisfies the requisite skill, experience, education, and other job-related requirements of the employment position such individual holds or desires, and who, with or without reasonable accommodation, can perform the essential functions of such position (II-11).

In other words, the applicant must still have the required knowledge, training, skill, and ability to perform the job. In addition, the law was not intended to interfere with the employer's right to hire the best qualified candidate or to establish appropriate job qualifications. Nonetheless, the law was intended to ensure that whatever requirements are set should not inappropriately exclude individuals with disability. For this reason, the ADA applies to all aspects of the selection processing including education and work experience requirements, physical and mental requirement, paper and pencil tests, safety requirements, physical and psychological tests, interview questions, and rating systems (IV-1).

If a job requirement would tend to screen out individuals with disabilities, then the employer is obligated to show that they requirement is both job related and consistent with business necessity. Job related requirements must be specifically related to the particular job not only to the general class of jobs. Similarly, a requirement can only be considered a business necessity if it is related to an *essential*, not marginal, function of a job.

WHAT ARE THE ESSENTIAL FUNCTIONS OF THE JOB?

As a rule, there is considerable discretion given to the employer in determining what the essential functions of a job are. However, the employer should not presume that just because something is identified as an essential function it will be considered as such. Supporting evidence for the employer might include a job description. Although the law does not require the existence of job descriptions, nor does it require that essential functions be identified in the descriptions, the use of a specific job description is important support when employment decisions are made. In addition, in conceptualizing an essential function, the employer should focus on the purpose and result (II-16) of the function and less on the method. That is, a disabled employee with reasonable accommodation (e.g., special equipment) might be able to accomplish the purpose of a particular function in a different way.

Functions can generally be considered essential if (II-13,14):

1. The position exists to perform the function; e.g., if one is requesting typing skills for a typist's position.

2. There are a limited number of employees to perform the function; e.g., an essential function for a library assistant may be to answer the telephone, especially if there are few employees in the workplace who are available to perform this function.

3. The function is highly specialized; e.g., if computer programming is required and the individual being considered must have this expertise.

4. A great deal of the employee's job is spent performing the task.

5. If the function, even if performed infrequently, must be performed well when needed.

It is also crucial that the function identified as essential is *actually* being performed in the job. Sometimes job descriptions contain tasks that are no longer performed. The inability of the candidate to perform such a task cannot be used to evaluate the adequacy of the candidate.

WHAT ARE REASONABLE ACCOMMODATIONS?

Once the essential functions of the job are identified, it remains the responsibility of the employer to determine if an otherwise qualified individual with a disability can perform these functions with reasonable accommodations. Reasonable accommodations are changes or alterations the employer makes that provide equal opportunity for an employee who is disabled. Reasonable accommodations are not required *unless* the individual is disabled. In addition, a distinguishing feature of the employment provisions of the ADA is that an employer is not required to make accommodations in the workplace until a particular individual requests this accommodation. That is, in terms of disabled employees, changes in the workplace are required only as they are needed.

Reasonable accommodations are made to assist the individual in three areas: to ensure that the candidate has a fair chance in the employment process, to assist disabled employees in performing the essential tasks of jobs, and to permit disabled employees to partake of the benefits and privileges of employment (III-2).

Reasonable accommodations include but are not restricted to the following (III-5,6):

- Making existing facilities used by employees readily accessible to, and usable by, an individual with a disability. This might involve installing ramps, removing thresholds, reserving parking spaces, making restrooms accessible, rearranging office furniture, making drinking fountains accessible, clearing "paths of travel" to equipment, meeting rooms and facilities, and adding flashing lights to warn individuals who are hearing impaired when emergencies exist.

- Restructuring a job by reallocating or redistributing marginal job functions. Only marginal functions are subject to changes. An employer is not required to reallocate essential functions. However, altering when or how an essential job function is performed could also be considered a reasonable accommodation.

- Permitting flexible or modified work schedules especially in regard to scheduling of medical treatment. This might also involve flexible leave policies for disabled workers, or allowing the use of accrued leave or leave without pay.

- Obtaining or modifying equipment or devices. Types of equipment that might be considered are telecommunication devices for the deaf (TDD), telephone amplifiers, Braille or raised print, telephone headsets, talking calculators, and speaker phones. The law does not require an employer to provide personal items such as glasses or hearing aids.

- Modifying examinations, training materials, or policies. This is required to ensure that the ability of the applicant is actually being measured rather than his or her disability. Use of oral versus written testing, and additional time to take the test may be reasonable accommodation. Generally, individuals should be given notice in advance that a test is being given so that accommodation can be requested.

- Providing qualified readers and interpreters. These may, for example, be required for visually or hearing impaired individuals insofar as the retention of a reader or interpreter does not cause undue hardship. In the hiring process, interpreters and readers may be needed in the application and interview process.

- Reassignment to a vacant position. This option is required only for currently employed individuals. For job applicants the employer is not required to consider other positions for which the applicant may be suitable.

- Allowing an employee to provide equipment or devices that an employer is not required to provide.

Generally, the employee or applicant is responsible for indicating if an accommodation is needed, and the employer need make an accommodation only if the individual is otherwise qualified for the position. The individual is not required to specifically request a "reasonable accommodation;" they need only ask for some change or alteration. If the disability is obvious, the employer may need to investigate reasonable accommodations, even if a specific request for such has not been forthcoming from the employee. In addition, the employer is responsible for notifying applicants and employees concerning the obligations of the employer to make accommodations to disabled workers. If an employee indicates she has a disability that requires accommodation, the employer has a right to request documentation of the disability including statements from physicians, or other professionals knowledgable of the disability.

In providing reasonable accommodations it is important to consult with the disabled individual and, when possible, provide the accommodation preferred by this individual. However, the employer is obligated only to provide an effective accommodation for the employee. Insofar as the accommodation permits the employee to perform the essential functions of the job, the employer is free to select the accommodation that is in the best interest of the employer (III-10).

UNDER WHAT CIRCUMSTANCES CAN AN EMPLOYER CLAIM THAT AN ACCOMMODATION IS UNREASONABLE?

The law does not require that an employer lower the standards of quality or quantity as a form of reasonable accommodation. If the employer believes that no reasonable accommodation can bring the disabled employee up to expected work standards, then the employer may refuse to hire the individual. In addition, an employer may consider whether the hiring of a disabled employee may pose a direct threat to the safety or health of the individual or others. In order for an employer to consider the safety or health risk, the employer must be able to show that the risk of "substantial harm" is significant, that the risk can be specifically identified, that the risk is actual and not merely based on speculation, that the seriousness of the risk is based on objective evidence, and that reasonable accommodation would not reduce the risk to an acceptable level (IV-9).

Perhaps the most common reason for refusal to accommodate is that the accommodation(s) needed would create what is called an "undue hardship" on the employer. "Undue hardship" under the ADA is defined as an accommodation that is:

... unduly costly, extensive, substantial, disruptive, or that would fundamentally alter the nature or operation of the business (III-12).

Among the factors to be considered in determining undue hardship are (1) the net costs of the accommodation, (2) the financial ability of the organization to pay for the accommodation, (3) the type of operation, structure, function, and administrative relationship of the facility to the larger organization, and (4) the impact of the accommodation. It is noteworthy that among the issues to be considered in analyzing the impact of an accommodation is the disruptive effect on other employees or on the organization to perform its function (III-14). A final factor that should be considered is the provisions of a collective bargaining agreement. If, for example, provisions for reassignment or transfer are circumscribed by union agreement, then accommodating disabled employees using these methods might pose serious hardship on the organization.

If undue hardship is claimed, the employer should give the disabled employee an opportunity to provide the accommodation by paying for it.

WHAT CAN YOU ASK IN AN INTERVIEW OR JOB APPLICATION FORM ABOUT A PERSON'S DISABILITY?

The job recruitment, application, interview, and selection process are all subject to scrutiny under the ADA. If the employer uses an employment agency to check references or screen candidates, it is essential that that agency also conform to the ADA or the employer may be held responsible.

RECRUITMENT

The ADA does not require that employers take special actions to recruit disabled employees, although taking aggressive action in this regard conforms to the spirit of the law. However, just like with other protected classes, recruitment strategies should not act to disproportionately screen out applicants with disabilities. Such strategies may be considered to be violations of the ADA.

When recruiting for positions, employers should identify the essential functions of the position in the job advertisement. If the job notice indicates a telephone number for further information about a job, the employer should consider a TDD number as well. Similarly, job information should be available in a form and at locations that are accessible to the disabled. This might involve preparing posted notices in large type, recording job information on a cassette, and insuring that the interviewing and application area is accessible by those in wheelchairs. If an employment agency is used as a recruitment source, the employer remains liable if the agency violates the provisions of the ADA in the recruitment of employees. It is not appropriate at the recruitment stage to make any inquiries regarding an individual's disabilities.

APPLICATION AND INTERVIEWING

As a rule, the applicant should not be asked during the application, interview, or reference checking process any questions about the existence, nature, or seriousness of a disability. The employer can explore whether the individual can perform particular job functions, but the employer should be careful not to frame the question in terms of a disability. Employers can ask an employee to demonstrate how she might perform a particular function with or without reasonable accommodation. Although this may not be a regular question in an interview, if the candidate has a known disability, the question may be asked even if other candidates are not asked this question (V-6). The application form should also contain a statement indicating that if an accommodation is needed in completing the application form or during an interview, that the employer should be notified. Accommodations might include changing the location so that it is accessible, providing a sign interpreter, or a reader for a blind applicant.

The following questions should *not* be asked on an application form or in a job interview (V-6):

- Have you ever had or been treated for any of the following conditions or diseases? (Followed by a checklist of various conditions and diseases.)

- Please list any conditions or diseases for which you have been treated in the past 3 years.

- Have you ever been hospitalized? If so, for what conditions?

- Have you ever been treated by a psychiatrist or psychologist? If so, for what condition?

- Have you ever been treated for any mental condition?

- Is there any health-related reason you may not be able to perform the job for which you are applying?

- Have you had a major illness in the last five years?

- How many days were you absent from work because of illness last year? (Note: an employer may provide information on its attendance requirements and ask if an applicant will be able to meet these requirements.)

- Do you have any physical defects which precludes you from performing certain kinds of work? If yes, describe such defects and specific work limitations.

- Do you have any disabilities or impairments which may affect your performance in the position for which you are applying? (Note: the applicant may be asked about ability to perform specific job functions, with or without a reasonable accommodation.)

- Are you taking any prescribed drugs?

- Have you ever been treated for drug addition or alcoholism?

- Have you ever filed for workers' compensation insurance?

Although direct questions about disabilities are not lawful under the ADA, during an interview an employer could provide a job description to the candidate are ask whether the individual could perform the tasks of the job and how they would perform these tasks, with or without reasonable accommodation. However, this type of question should be asked of all candidates, unless the candidate has a *known* disability at which point the question may be asked just of that candidate (V-14). Attendance records may be queried in an interview and on an application form but only if there is *no* reference to a disability.

JOB TESTS

The use of tests are not prohibited under the ADA; however, it is essential that whatever tests are used, they do not disproportionately screen out individuals with a disability. Tests are broadly construed under the ADA and include those that measure aptitude, knowledge, intelligence, and agility. They also include job demonstration tests.

If a test is shown to screen out individuals because of their disabilities, then it must be shown to be job-related and consistent with business necessity. Even if job-relatedness and business necessity are demonstrated, it is still necessary to offer a reasonable accommodation. Among the possible reasonable accommodations might be (V-15):

- making the test site accessible for individuals with mobility problems,
- substituting written for oral tests or visa versa,
- providing a reader,
- administering a test in large print or in Braille,
- allowing answers to be recorded on tape,
- scheduling rest breaks during testing,
- use other means besides a test to determine if the candidate has the required knowledge, skill and ability, and
- providing extra time during the test.

Before a test is given, the applicant should be forewarned that a test is part of the hiring process and should be given the opportunity to request an accommodation. It is generally the applicant's responsibility to request the accommodation once notified that a test will be given.

PHYSICAL EXAMINATIONS

An employer can make a job offer conditional on the satisfactory results of a medical examination. Drug tests to determine the unlawful use of drugs are not prohibited under the ADA. A medical examination can occur only *after* the offer has been made. It is essential, however, that if an employer uses medical exams for disabled employees, that the same examinations be conducted of all employees *in the same job category*. However, the medical examinations do not have to be identical. The identification of a physical or mental problem may require additional tests not conducted of all employees in the same job category. In addition, the reason for the exam must be job-related and consistent with business necessity, and a refusal to hire can only be made if no reasonable accommodation would allow the individual to perform the essential functions of the job. This highlights the fact that the doctor's statement should focus on the employee's ability to perform the essential functions of the job with or without accommodation, and whether performing the tasks would pose a direct threat to the health and safety of the employee or others. *The results of medical examinations should be treated as confidential medical records and stored in locked cabinets apart from the personnel files.* Only specified individuals should have access to these files. The information in such files should be severely limited. Examples of type of information that might be disseminated from these files might include informing supervisors of restrictions on work duties of an employee or identifying the reasonable accommodation needed to assist a disabled employee. Similarly, key personnel might be informed what types of emergency measures might be required for a particular disability.

A medical examination may also be required of currently employed individuals if they have recently become disabled, or if an employee is no longer performing the job effectively. In any case, the same obligations to focus on job-related abilities consistent with business necessity and to provide reasonable accommodation remain.

HOW ARE PAY AND HEALTH BENEFITS AFFECTED?

An offer to hire an individual with a disability should be made under the same terms and conditions for individuals without disabilities. The employer cannot offer a lower salary because of the disability or the cost of the accommodation made, nor may the employer reduce salary because marginal aspects of the job have been removed. However, if a disabled employee is moved to another position because the disability makes it impossible to perform the essential functions of the current job, the employee may be compensated at the rate appropriate for the new position even if it is a lower rate.

Similarly, the same health benefits must be offered to the disabled individual as to other employees without a disability. Employers should especially note that they cannot refuse to hire an individual because of the belief that the employee's disability, or the disability of a family member, may affect the employer's future health care costs. The ADA, however, does permit health insurance plans to reflect the regular principles of risk assessment. This means that health plans can still have such features as pre-existing conditions, and may restrict coverage for certain procedures or treatments, even if it tends to adversely affect individuals with disabilities (VII-9).

WHO ENFORCES THE ADA?

The U.S. Equal Employment Opportunity Commission (EEOC) is responsible for enforcing the employment provisions of the ADA. It is essential for employers to note that the remedies for this law are considerable. A plaintiff may seek compensatory and punitive damages, back pay, front pay, restored benefits, attorney's fees, reasonable accommodation, reinstatement and job offers. It is the responsibility of employers to notify their employees of their rights under the ADA through the posting of notices which are accessible to all employees including those with visual and other disabilities.

DEALING WITH THE ADA

It is understandable that employers may sometimes feel that they are inundated with laws and regulations that make personnel management, including the hiring process, into an unnecessarily difficult task. It is true that laws such as the ADA increase the burden on the employer to ensure that hiring processes are scrupulously fair. But employers should also see the ADA as a special opportunity: an opportunity to recruit and retain a category of potential employees who are an untapped resource. Today, a disproportionate percentage of individuals with disabilities are unemployed. They in fact represent a significant workforce of productive workers whose talents have yet to be properly used. The ADA has caused employers to focus on this group, and in these early years, libraries have a chance to draw from this substantial labor pool and to recruit and retain some excellent workers. Rather than attempting to find ways to circumvent the ADA, library employers should be aggressively recruiting from this labor pool. By seeking out qualified applicants, the library takes control of the situation and increases its chances of getting the right individual for the job.

Locating the appropriate sources for disabled workers and learning by what means the workplace can respond to these individuals may require some outside assistance. On the Federal level, the Equal Employment Opportunity Commission has issued the *Resource Directory for the Americans With Disabilities Act* which provides information on Federal and non-governmental agencies including agencies within the various states that can assist in this activity.[2]

REFERENCES

1. Equal Employment Opportunity Commission. *Technical Assistance Manual for the Americans With Disabilities Act.* Boston: Warren, Gorham and Lamont, 1992.

2. Equal Employment Opportunity Commission. *Resource Directory for the Americans With Disabilities Act.* Boston: Warren, Gorham and Lamont, 1992.

8 CONCLUDING REMARKS

Libraries are labor-intensive organizations: they depend on people to perform their essential functions. The constituencies of libraries rely heavily on library staff to serve them professionally and well. What libraries do is very important, and the library administrator has a considerable burden to hire individuals who provide excellent service. The library is, with rare exceptions, a public trust. It is not the duty of libraries to provide continued employment to those who are unproductive; to the contrary it is the duty of library administrators to hire and retain highly productive and well-motivated employees.

This is a great burden on the employer because of the complexity of the process and the potential effects on the organization each time a new employee is hired. The work environment is a complex place. It is not only a place where people perform defined functions; it is a place where people interact. These interactions may be among staff and patrons or among staff members themselves. Each new employee introduces a new dynamic into the job situation. A single poor selection can create serious consequences not only in terms of ineffective service, but declines in morale and increases in legal liabilities. The importance of the hiring process can, therefore, not be overestimated.

For this reason, the hiring process must be seen as broader than finding an individual with particular skills for a particular job; the process must find a match or fit between the applicant and the job. This match not only is defined by the job tasks, but the work environment and culture of the organization.

The hiring process is really an attempt to locate individuals who are willing to become members of the organization and who will be happy and productive working within the organization. It is a matching process in which the dispositions, talents, abilities, and needs of individuals are matched with the needs of the organization.

Below are 20 questions that administrators should ask themselves when reviewing their organization's hiring policies and procedures:

1. Do I have clearly written hiring policies and procedures and are these policies and procedures followed scrupulously?
2. Do I have a job application form that provides me with the essential, job-related information for screening candidates?

3. Do I have adequate provisions for handling candidates with disabilities?
4. Are my job descriptions carefully prepared and up-to-date?
5. Is there adequate training for my selectors?
6. Are all candidates treated equally in the hiring process?
7. Can my selectors clearly state what the essential functions of a position are when it is open?
8. Am I getting an ample supply of applications when a job opens and are applicants generally of good quality?
9. Do candidates have a good impression of the organization as they go through the hiring process?
10. Do I have a systematic method of checking references?
11. Are the job interviews structured?
12. Is the selection criteria based on the demands of the position?
13. Are my selectors able to articulate clearly the job-related reasons why they are making a particular job choice?
14. Are the employees that I hire productive workers?
15. Do the employees that I hire leave soon after they are hired?
16. Are my selectors aware of the legal requirements of the hiring process?
17. Does it take an excessively long time to fill a position?
18. Is there a clearly defined process for orienting and training employees after they are hired?
19. Do I have a means of monitoring the hiring process to ensure equal employment opportunity?
20. Am I getting complaints from the public or staff about my hiring practices?

In the final analysis, the quality of a library administrator may, in large part, be judged on the quality of the staff. It is the library director who must be held responsible when library staff is ineffective. It is right and proper that hiring good employees must be considered an essential accountability of the chief administrator, regardless of the extent to which that responsibility is delegated. It is for this reason that a systematic and intelligent hiring system must be part of any well-run library. The risks and rewards are too great to leave the selection of employees to chance.

APPENDIX A

UNIFORM GUIDELINES ON EMPLOYEE SELECTION PROCEDURES

tion of the rule as evidence of discrimination on the basis of national origin.

§ 1606.8 Harassment.

(a) The Commission has consistently held that harassment on the basis of national origin is a violation of Title VII. An employer has an affirmative duty to maintain a working environment free of harassment on the basis of national origin.[*]

(b) Ethnic slurs and other verbal or physical conduct relating to an individual's national origin constitute harassment when this conduct: (1) Has the purpose or effect of creating an intimidating, hostile or offensive working environment; (2) has the purpose or effect of unreasonably interfering with an individual's work performance; or (3) otherwise adversely affects an individual's employment opportunities.

(c) An employer is responsible for its acts and those of its agents and supervisory employees with respect to harassment on the basis of national origin regardless of whether the specific acts complained of were authorized or even forbidden by the employer and regardless of whether the employer knew or should have known of their occurrence. The Commission will examine the circumstances of the particular employment relationship and the job functions performed by the individual in determining whether an individual acts in either a supervisory or agency capacity.

(d) With respect to conduct between fellow employees, an employer is responsible for acts of harassment in the workplace on the basis of national origin, where the employer, its agents or supervisory employees, knows or should have known of the conduct, unless the employer can show that it took immediate and appropriate corrective action.

(e) An employer may also be responsible for the acts of non-employees with respect to harassment of employees in the workplace on the basis of national origin, where the employer, its agents or supervisory employees, knows or should have known of the conduct and fails to take immediate and appropriate corrective action. In reviewing these cases, the Commission will consider the extent of the employer's control and any other legal responsibility which the employer may have with respect to the conduct of such non-employees.

PART 1607—UNIFORM GUIDELINES ON EMPLOYEE SELECTION PROCEDURES (1978)

COMPREHENSIVE TABLE OF CONTENTS

GENERAL PRINCIPLES

---

[*]See CD CL68-12-431 EU (1969), CCH EEOC Decisions ¶6085, 2 FEP Cases 295; CD 72-0621 (1971), CCH EEOC Decisions ¶6311, 4 FEP Cases 312; CD 72-1561 (1972), CCH EEOC Decisions ¶6354, 4 FEP Cases 852; CD 74-05 (1973), CCH EEOC Decisions ¶6387, 6 FEP Cases 834; CD 76-41 (1975), CCH EEOC Decisions ¶6632. See also, Amendment to *Guidelines on Discrimination Because of Sex*, § 1604.11(a) n. 1, 45 FR 7476 sy 74677 (November 10, 1980).

Equal Employment Opportunity Comm.

E. Accuracy and Standardization

F. Caution Against Selection on Basis of Knowledges, Skills or Abilities Learned in Brief Orientation Period

G. Method of Use of Selection Procedures

H. Cutoff Scores

I. Use of Selection Procedures for Higher Level Jobs

J. Interim Use of Selection Procedures

K. Review of Validity Studies for Currency

1607.6. Use of Selection Procedures Which Have Not Been Validated

A. Use of Alternate Selection Procedures to Eliminate Adverse Impact

B. Where Validity Studies Cannot or Need Not Be Performed

(1) Where Informal or Unscored Procedures Are Used

(2) Where Formal And Scored Procedures Are Used

1607.7. Use of Other Validity Studies

A. Validity Studies not Conducted by the User

B. Use of Criterion-Related Validity Evidence from Other Sources

(1) Validity Evidence

(2) Job Similarity

(3) Fairness Evidence

C. Validity Evidence from Multi-Unit Study

D. Other Significant Variables

1607.8. Cooperative Studies

A. Encouragement of Cooperative Studies

B. Standards for Use of Cooperative Studies

1607.9. No Assumption of Validity

A. Unacceptable Substitutes for Evidence of Validity

B. Encouragement of Professional Supervision

1607.10. Employment Agencies and Employment Services

A. Where Selection Procedures Are Devised by Agency

B. Where Selection Procedures Are Devised Elsewhere

1607.11. Disparate Treatment

1607.12. Retesting of Applicants

1607.13. Affirmative Action

A. Affirmative Action Obligations

B. Encouragement of Voluntary Affirmative Action Programs

TECHNICAL STANDARDS

1607.14. Technical Standards for Validity Studies

A. Validity Studies Should be Based on Review of Information about the Job

B. Technical Standards for Criterion-Related Validity Studies

(1) Technical Feasibility

(2) Analysis of the Job

(3) Criterion Measures

(4) Representativeness of the Sample

(5) Statistical Relationships

(6) Operational Use of Selection Procedures

(7) Over-Statement of Validity Findings

(8) Fairness

(a) Unfairness Defined

(b) Investigation of Fairness

(c) General Considerations in Fairness Investigations

(d) When Unfairness Is Shown

(e) Technical Feasibility of Fairness Studies

(f) Continued Use of Selection Procedures When Fairness Studies not Feasible

C. Technical Standards for Content Validity Studies

(1) Appropriateness of Content Validity Studies

(2) Job Analysis for Content Validity

(3) Development of Selection Procedure

(4) Standards For Demonstrating Content Validity

(5) Reliability

(6) Prior Training or Experience

(7) Training Success

(8) Operational Use

(9) Ranking Based on Content Validity Studies

D. Technical Standards For Construct Validity Studies

(1) Appropriateness of Construct Validity Studies

(2) Job Analysis For Construct Validity Studies

(3) Relationship to the Job

(4) Use of Construct Validity Study Without New Criterion-Related Evidence

(a) Standards for Use

(b) Determination of Common Work Behaviors

DOCUMENTATION OF IMPACT AND VALIDITY EVIDENCE

1607.15. Documentation of Impact and Validity Evidence

A. Required Information

(1) Simplified Recordkeeping for Users With Less Than 100 Employees

(2) Information on Impact

(a) Collection of Information on Impact

(b) When Adverse Impact Has Been Eliminated in The Total Selection Process

(c) When Data Insufficient to Determine Impact

(3) Documentation of Validity Evidence

(a) Type of Evidence

(b) Form of Report

(c) Completeness

B. Criterion-Related Validity Studies

(1) User(s), Location(s), and Date(s) of Study

(2) Problem and Setting

(3) Job Analysis or Review of Job Information

§ 1607.1

AUTHORITY: Secs. 709 and 713, Civil Rights Act of 1964 (78 Stat. 265) as amended by the Equal Employment Opportunity Act of 1972 (Pub. L. 92-261); 42 U.S.C. 2000c-8, 2000c-12.

SOURCE: 43 FR 38295 and 43 FR 38312, Aug. 25, 1978, unless otherwise noted.

GENERAL PRINCIPLES

§ 1607.1 Statement of purpose.

A. *Need for uniformity—Issuing agencies.* The Federal government's need for a uniform set of principles on the question of the use of tests and other selection procedures has long been recognized. The Equal Employment Opportunity Commission, the Civil Service Commission, the Department of Labor, and the Department of Justice jointly have adopted these uniform guidelines to meet that need, and to apply the same principles to the Federal Government as are applied to other employers.

B. *Purpose of guidelines.* These guidelines incorporate a single set of principles which are designed to assist employers, labor organizations, employment agencies, and licensing and certification boards to comply with requirements of Federal law prohibiting employment practices which discriminate on grounds of race, color, religion, sex, and national origin. They are designed to provide a framework for determining the proper use of tests and other selection procedures. These guidelines do not require a user to conduct validity studies of selection procedures where no adverse impact results. However, all users are encouraged to use selection procedures which are valid, especially users operating under merit principles.

C. *Relation to prior guidelines.* These guidelines are based upon and supersede previously issued guidelines on employee selection procedures. These guidelines have been built upon court decisions, the previously issued guidelines of the agencies, and the practical experience of the agencies, as well as the standards of the psychological profession. These guidelines are intended to be consistent with existing law.

§ 1607.2 Scope.

A. *Application of guidelines.* These guidelines will be applied by the Equal Employment Opportunity Commission in the enforcement of title VII of the Civil Rights Act of 1964, as amended by the Equal Employment Opportunity Act of 1972 (hereinafter "Title VII"); by the Department of Labor, and the contract compliance agencies until the transfer of authority contemplated by the President's Reorganization Plan No. 1 of 1978, in the administration and enforcement of Executive Order 11246, as amended by Executive Order 11375 (hereinafter "Executive Order 11246"); by the Civil Service Commission and other Federal agencies subject to section 717 of Title VII; by the Civil Service Commission in exercising its responsibilities toward State and local governments under section 208(b)(1) of the Intergovernmental-Personnel Act; by the Department of Justice in exercising its responsibilities under Federal law; by the Office of Revenue Sharing of the Department of the Treasury under the State and Local Fiscal Assistance Act of 1972, as amended; and by any other Federal agency which adopts them.

B. *Employment decisions.* These guidelines apply to tests and other selection procedures which are used as a basis for any employment decision. Employment decisions include but are not limited to hiring, promotion, demotion, membership (for example, in a labor organization), referral, retention, and licensing and certification, to the extent that licensing and certification may be covered by Federal equal employment opportunity law. Other selection decisions, such as selection for training or transfer, may also be considered employment decisions if they lead to any of the decisions listed above.

C. *Selection procedures.* These guidelines apply only to selection procedures which are used as a basis for making employment decisions. For example, the use of recruiting procedures designed to attract members of a particular race, sex, or ethnic group, which were previously denied employment opportunities or which are currently underutilized, may be necessary to bring an employer into compliance with Federal law, and is frequently an essential element of any effective affirmative action program; but recruitment practices are not considered by these guidelines to be selection proce-

dures. Similarly, these guidelines do not pertain to the question of the lawfulness of a seniority system within the meaning of section 703(h), Executive Order 11246 or other provisions of Federal law or regulation, except to the extent that such systems utilize selection procedures to determine qualifications or abilities to perform the job. Nothing in these guidelines is intended or should be interpreted as discouraging the use of a selection procedure for the purpose of determining qualifications or for the purpose of selection on the basis of relative qualifications, if the selection procedure had been validated in accord with these guidelines for each such purpose for which it is to be used.

D. *Limitations.* These guidelines apply only to persons subject to Title VII, Executive Order 11246, or other equal employment opportunity requirements of Federal law. These guidelines do not apply to responsibilities under the Age Discrimination in Employment Act of 1967, as amended, not to discriminate on the basis of age, or under sections 501, 503, and 504 of the Rehabilitation Act of 1973, not to discriminate on the basis of handicap.

E. *Indian preference not affected.* These guidelines do not restrict any obligation imposed or right granted by Federal law to users to extend a preference in employment to Indians living on or near an Indian reservation in connection with employment opportunities on or near an Indian reservation.

§1607.3 Discrimination defined: Relationship between use of selection procedures and discrimination.

A. *Procedure having adverse impact constitutes discrimination unless justified.* The use of any selection procedure which has an adverse impact on the hiring, promotion, or other employment or membership opportunities of members of any race, sex, or ethnic group will be considered to be discriminatory and inconsistent with these guidelines, unless the procedure has been validated in accordance with these guidelines, or the provisions of section 6 below are satisfied.

B. *Consideration of suitable alternative selection procedures.* Where two or more selection procedures are available which serve the user's legitimate interest in efficient and trustworthy workmanship, and which are substantially equally valid for a given purpose, the user should use the procedure which has been demonstrated to have the lesser adverse impact. Accordingly, whenever a validity study is called for by these guidelines, the user should include, as a part of the validity study, an investigation of suitable alternative selection procedures and suitable alternative methods of using the selection procedure which have as little adverse impact as possible, to determine the appropriateness of using or validating them in accord with these guidelines. If a user has made a reasonable effort to become aware of such alternative procedures and validity has been demonstrated in accord with these guidelines, the use of the test or other selection procedure may continue until such time as it should reasonably be reviewed for currency. Whenever the user is shown an alternative selection procedure with evidence of less adverse impact and substantial evidence of validity for the same job in similar circumstances, the user should investigate it to determine the appropriateness of using or validating it in accord with these guidelines. This subsection is not intended to preclude the combination of procedures into a significantly more valid procedure, if the use of such a combination has been shown to be in compliance with the guidelines.

§ 1607.4 Information on impact.

A. *Records concerning impact.* Each user should maintain and have available for inspection records or other information which will disclose the impact which its tests and other selection procedures have upon employment opportunities of persons by identifiable race, sex, or ethnic group as set forth in subparagraph B below in order to determine compliance with these guidelines. Where there are large numbers of applicants and procedures are administered frequently, such information may be retained on a sample basis, provided that the sample

is appropriate in terms of the applicant population and adequate in size.

B. *Applicable race, sex, and ethnic groups for recordkeeping.* The records called for by this section are to be maintained by sex, and the following races and ethnic groups: Blacks (Negroes), American Indians (including Alaskan Natives), Asians (including Pacific Islanders), Hispanic (including persons of Mexican, Puerto Rican, Cuban, Central or South American, or other Spanish origin or culture regardless of race), whites (Caucasians) other than Hispanic, and totals. The race, sex, and ethnic classifications called for by this section are consistent with the Equal Employment Opportunity Standard Form 100, Employer Information Report EEO-1 series of reports. The user should adopt safeguards to insure that the records required by this paragraph are used for appropriate purposes such as determining adverse impact, or (where required) for developing and monitoring affirmative action programs, and that such records are not used improperly. See sections 4E and 17(4), below.

C. *Evaluation of selection rates. The "bottom line."* If the information called for by sections 4A and B above shows that the total selection process for a job has an adverse impact, the individual components of the selection process should be evaluated for adverse impact. If this information shows that the total selection process does not have an adverse impact, the Federal enforcement agencies, in the exercise of their administrative and prosecutorial discretion, in usual circumstances, will not expect a user to evaluate the individual components for adverse impact, or to validate such individual components, and will not take enforcement action based upon adverse impact of any component of that process, including the separate parts of a multipart selection procedure or any separate procedure that is used as an alternative method of selection. However, in the following circumstances the Federal enforcement agencies will expect a user to evaluate the individual components for adverse impact and may, where appropriate, take enforcement action with respect to the individual components: (1)

Equal Employment Opportunity Comm.

Where the selection procedure is a significant factor in the continuation of patterns of assignments of incumbent employees caused by prior discriminatory employment practices, (2) where the weight of court decisions or administrative interpretations hold that a specific procedure (such as height or weight requirements or no-arrest records) is not job related in the same or similar circumstances. In unusual circumstances, other than those listed in (1) and (2) above, the Federal enforcement agencies may request a user to evaluate the individual components for adverse impact and may, where appropriate, take enforcement action with respect to the individual component.

D. *Adverse impact and the "four-fifths rule."* A selection rate for any race, sex, or ethnic group which is less than four-fifths (⅘) (or eighty percent) of the rate for the group with the highest rate will generally be regarded by the Federal enforcement agencies as evidence of adverse impact, while a greater than four-fifths rate will generally not be regarded by Federal enforcement agencies as evidence of adverse impact. Smaller differences in selection rate may nevertheless constitute adverse impact, where they are significant in both statistical and practical terms or where a user's actions have discouraged applicants disproportionately on grounds of race, sex, or ethnic group. Greater differences in selection rate may not constitute adverse impact where the differences are based on small numbers and are not statistically significant, or where special recruiting or other programs cause the pool of minority or female candidates to be atypical of the normal pool of applicants from that group. Where the user's evidence concerning the impact of a selection procedure indicates adverse impact but is based upon numbers which are too small to be reliable, evidence concerning the impact of the procedure over a longer period of time and/or evidence concerning the impact which the selection procedure had when used in the same manner in similar circumstances elsewhere may be considered in determining adverse impact. Where the user has not maintained data on adverse impact as required by the documentation section of applicable guidelines, the Federal enforcement agencies may draw an inference of adverse impact of the selection process from the failure of the user to maintain such data, if the user has an underutilization of a group in the job category, as compared to the group's representation in the relevant labor market or, in the case of jobs filled from within, the applicable work force.

E. *Consideration of user's equal employment opportunity posture.* In carrying out their obligations, the Federal enforcement agencies will consider the general posture of the user with respect to equal employment opportunity for the job or group of jobs in question. Where a user has adopted an affirmative action program, the Federal enforcement agencies will consider the provisions of that program, including the goals and timetables which the user has adopted and the progress which the user has made in carrying out that program and in meeting the goals and timetables. While such affirmative action programs may in design and execution be race, color, sex, or ethnic conscious, selection procedures under such programs should be based upon the ability or relative ability to do the work.

(Approved by the Office of Management and Budget under control number 3046-0017)

(Pub. L. No. 96-511, 94 Stat. 2812 (44 U.S.C. 3501 et seq.))

[43 FR 38295, 38312, Aug. 25, 1978, as amended at 46 FR 63268, Dec. 31, 1981]

§ 1607.5 General standards for validity studies.

A. *Acceptable types of validity studies.* For the purposes of satisfying these guidelines, users may rely upon criterion-related validity studies, content validity studies or construct validity studies, in accordance with the standards set forth in the technical standards of these guidelines, section 14 below. New strategies for showing the validity of selection procedures will be evaluated as they become accepted by the psychological profession.

B. *Criterion-related, content, and construct validity.* Evidence of the validity of a test or other selection procedure by a criterion-related validity study should consist of empirical data demonstrating that the selection procedure is predictive of or significantly correlated with important elements of job performance. See section 14B below. Evidence of the validity of a test or other selection procedure by a content validity study should consist of data showing that the content of the selection procedure is representative of important aspects of performance on the job for which the candidates are to be evaluated. See 14C below. Evidence of the validity of a test or other selection procedure through a construct validity study should consist of data showing that the procedure measures the degree to which candidates have identifiable characteristics which have been determined to be important in successful performance in the job for which the candidates are to be evaluated. See section 14D below.

C. *Guidelines are consistent with professional standards.* The provisions of these guidelines relating to validation of selection procedures are intended to be consistent with generally accepted professional standards for evaluating standardized tests and other selection procedures, such as those described in the Standards for Educational and Psychological Tests prepared by a joint committee of the American Psychological Association, the American Educational Research Association, and the National Council on Measurement in Education (American Psychological Association, Washington, D.C., 1974) (hereinafter "A.P.A. Standards") and standard textbooks and journals in the field of personnel selection.

D. *Need for documentation of validity.* For any selection procedure which is part of a selection process which has an adverse impact and which selection procedure has an adverse impact, each user should maintain and have available such documentation as is described in section 15 below.

E. *Accuracy and standardization.* Validity studies should be carried out under conditions which assure insofar as possible the adequacy and accuracy of the research and the report. Selection procedures should be administered and scored under standardized conditions.

F. *Caution against selection on basis of knowledges, skills, or ability learned in brief orientation period.* In general, users should avoid making employment decisions on the basis of measures of knowledges, skills, or abilities which are normally learned in a brief orientation period, and which have an adverse impact.

G. *Method of use of selection procedures.* The evidence of both the validity and utility of a selection procedure should support the method the user chooses for operational use of the procedure, if that method of use has a greater adverse impact than another method of use. Evidence which may be sufficient to support the use of a selection procedure on a pass/fail (screening) basis may be insufficient to support the use of the same procedure on a ranking basis under these guidelines. Thus, if a user decides to use a selection procedure on a ranking basis, and that method of use has a greater adverse impact than use on an appropriate pass/fail basis (see section 5H below), the user should have sufficient evidence of validity and utility to support the use on a ranking basis. See sections 3B, 14B (5) and (6), and 14C (8) and (9).

H. *Cutoff scores.* Where cutoff scores are used, they should normally be set so as to be reasonable and consistent with normal expectations of acceptable proficiency within the work force. Where applicants are ranked on the basis of properly validated selection procedures and those applicants scoring below a higher cutoff score than appropriate in light of such expectations have little or no chance of being selected for employment, the higher cutoff score may be appropriate, but the degree of adverse impact should be considered.

I. *Use of selection procedures for higher level jobs.* If job progression structures are so established that employees will probably, within a reasonable period of time and in a majority of cases, progress to a higher level, it may be considered that the applicants

Equal Employment Opportunity Comm. § 1607.6

are being evaluated for a job or jobs at the higher level. However, where job progression is not so nearly automatic, or the time span is such that higher level jobs or employees' potential may be expected to change in significant ways, it should be considered that applicants are being evaluated for a job at or near the entry level. A "reasonable period of time" will vary for different jobs and employment situations but will seldom be more than 5 years. Use of selection procedures to evaluate applicants for a higher level job would not be appropriate:

(1) If the majority of those remaining employed do not progress to the higher level job;

(2) If there is a reason to doubt that the higher level job will continue to require essentially similar skills during the progression period; or

(3) If the selection procedures measure knowledges, skills, or abilities required for advancement which would be expected to develop principally from the training or experience on the job.

J. *Interim use of selection procedures.* Users may continue the use of a selection procedure which is not at the moment fully supported by the required evidence of validity, provided: (1) The user has available substantial evidence of validity, and (2) the user has in progress, when technically feasible, a study which is designed to produce the additional evidence required by these guidelines within a reasonable time. If such a study is not technically feasible, see section 6B. If the study does not demonstrate validity, this provision of these guidelines for interim use shall not constitute a defense in any action, nor shall it relieve the user of any obligations arising under Federal law.

K. *Review of validity studies for currency.* Whenever validity has been shown in accord with these guidelines for the use of a particular selection procedure for a job or group of jobs, additional studies need not be performed until such time as the validity study is subject to review as provided in section 3B above. There are no absolutes in the area of determining the currency of a validity study. All circumstances concerning the study, in-

cluding the validation strategy used, and changes in the relevant labor market and the job should be considered in the determination of when a validity study is outdated.

§ 1607.6 Use of selection procedures which have not been validated.

A. *Use of alternate selection procedures to eliminate adverse impact.* A user may choose to utilize alternative selection procedures in order to eliminate adverse impact or as part of an affirmative action program. See section 13 below. Such alternative procedures should eliminate the adverse impact in the total selection process, should be lawful and should be as job related as possible.

B. *Where validity studies cannot or need not be performed.* There are circumstances in which a user cannot or need not utilize the validation techniques contemplated by these guidelines. In such circumstances, the user should utilize selection procedures which are as job related as possible and which will minimize or eliminate adverse impact, as set forth below.

(1) *Where informal or unscored procedures are used.* When an informal or unscored selection procedure which has an adverse impact is utilized, the user should eliminate the adverse impact, or modify the procedure to one which is a formal, scored or quantified measure or combination of measures and then validate the procedure in accord with these guidelines, or otherwise justify continued use of the procedure in accord with Federal law.

(2) *Where formal and scored procedures are used.* When a formal and scored selection procedure is used which has an adverse impact, the validation techniques contemplated by these guidelines usually should be followed if technically feasible. Where the user cannot or need not follow the validation techniques anticipated by these guidelines, the user should either modify the procedure to eliminate adverse impact or otherwise justify continued use of the procedure in accord with Federal law.

§ 1607.7 Use of other validity studies.

A. *Validity studies not conducted by the user.* Users may, under certain circumstances, support the use of selection procedures by validity studies conducted by other users or conducted by test publishers or distributors and described in test manuals. While publishers of selection procedures have a professional obligation to provide evidence of validity which meets generally accepted professional standards (see section 5C above), users are cautioned that they are responsible for compliance with these guidelines. Accordingly, users seeking to obtain selection procedures from publishers and distributors should be careful to determine that, in the event the user becomes subject to the validity requirements of these guidelines, the necessary information to support validity has been determined and will be made available to the user.

B. *Use of criterion-related validity evidence from other sources.* Criterion-related validity studies conducted by one test user, or described in test manuals and the professional literature, will be considered acceptable for use by another user when the following requirements are met:

(1) *Validity evidence.* Evidence from the available studies meeting the standards of section 14B below clearly demonstrates that the selection procedure is valid;

(2) *Job similarity.* The incumbents in the user's job and the incumbents in the job or group of jobs on which the validity study was conducted perform substantially the same major work behaviors, as shown by appropriate job analyses both on the job or group of jobs on which the validity study was performed and on the job for which the selection procedure is to be used; and

(3) *Fairness evidence.* The studies include a study of test fairness for each race, sex, and ethnic group which constitutes a significant factor in the borrowing user's relevant labor market for the job or jobs in question. If the studies under consideration satisfy (1) and (2) above but do not contain an investigation of test fairness, and it is not technically feasible for the borrowing user to conduct an internal study of test fairness, the borrowing user may utilize the study until studies conducted elsewhere meeting the requirements of these guidelines show test unfairness, or until such time as it becomes technically feasible to conduct an internal study of test fairness and the results of that study can be acted upon. Users obtaining selection procedures from publishers should consider, as one factor in the decision to purchase a particular selection procedure, the availability of evidence concerning test fairness.

C. *Validity evidence from multiunit study.* If validity evidence from a study covering more than one unit within an organization statisfies the requirements of section 14B below, evidence of validity specific to each unit will not be required unless there are variables which are likely to affect validity significantly.

D. *Other significant variables.* If there are variables in the other studies which are likely to affect validity significantly, the user may not rely upon such studies, but will be expected either to conduct an internal validity study or to comply with section 6 above.

§ 1607.8 Cooperative studies.

A. *Encouragement of cooperative studies.* The agencies issuing these guidelines encourage employers, labor organizations, and employment agencies to cooperate in research, development, search for lawful alternatives, and validity studies in order to achieve procedures which are consistent with these guidelines.

B. *Standards for use of cooperative studies.* If validity evidence from a cooperative study satisfies the requirements of section 14 below, evidence of validity specific to each user will not be required unless there are variables in the user's situation which are likely to affect validity significantly.

§ 1607.9 No assumption of validity.

A. *Unacceptable substitutes for evidence of validity.* Under no circumstances will the general reputation of a test or other selection procedures, its author or its publisher, or casual reports of it's validity be accepted in lieu

Equal Employment Opportunity Comm. §1607.12

of evidence of validity. Specifically ruled out are: assumptions of validity based on a procedure's name or descriptive labels; all forms of promotional literature; data bearing on the frequency of a procedure's usage; testimonial statements and credentials of sellers, users, or consultants; and other nonempirical or anecdotal accounts of selection practices or selection outcomes.

B. *Encouragement of professional supervision.* Professional supervision of selection activities is encouraged but is not a substitute for documented evidence of validity. The enforcement agencies will take into account the fact that a thorough job analysis was conducted and that careful development and use of a selection procedure in accordance with professional standards enhance the probability that the selection procedure is valid for the job.

§1607.10 Employment agencies and employment services.

A. *Where selection procedures are devised by agency.* An employment agency, including private employment agencies and State employment agencies, which agrees to a request by an employer or labor organization to device and utilize a selection procedure should follow the standards in these guidelines for determining adverse impact. If adverse impact exists the agency should comply with these guidelines. An employment agency is not relieved of its obligation herein because the user did not request such validation or has requested the use of some lesser standard of validation than is provided in these guidelines. The use of an employment agency does not relieve an employer or labor organization or other user of its responsibilities under Federal law to provide equal employment opportunity or its obligations as a user under these guidelines.

B. *Where selection procedures are devised elsewhere.* Where an employment agency or service is requested to administer a selection procedure which has been devised elsewhere and to make referrals pursuant to the results, the employment agency or service should maintain and have available evidence of the impact of the selection and referral procedures which it administers. If adverse impact results the agency or service should comply with these guidelines. If the agency or service seeks to comply with these guidelines by reliance upon validity studies or other data in the possession of the employer, it should obtain and have available such information.

§1607.11 Disparate treatment.

The principles of disparate or unequal treatment must be distinguished from the concepts of validation. A selection procedure—even though validated against job performance in accordance with these guidelines—cannot be imposed upon members of a race, sex, or ethnic group where other employees, applicants, or members have not been subjected to that standard. Disparate treatment occurs where members of a race, sex, or ethnic group have been denied the same employment, promotion, membership, or other employment opportunities as have been available to other employees or applicants. Those employees or applicants who have been denied equal treatment, because of prior discriminatory practices or policies, must at least be afforded the same opportunities as had existed for other employees or applicants during the period of discrimination. Thus, the persons who were in the class of persons discriminated against during the period the user followed the discriminatory practices should be allowed the opportunity to qualify under less stringent selection procedures previously followed, unless the user demonstrates that the increased standards are required by business necessity. This section does not prohibit a user who has not previously followed merit standards from adopting merit standards which are in compliance with these guidelines; nor does it preclude a user who has previously used invalid or unvalidated selection procedures from developing and using procedures which are in accord with these guidelines.

§1607.12 Retesting of applicants.

Users should provide a reasonable opportunity for retesting and reconsideration. Where examinations are

§ 1607.13

administered periodically with public notice, such reasonable opportunity exists, unless persons who have previously been tested are precluded from retesting. The user may however take reasonable steps to preserve the security of its procedures.

§ 1607.13 Affirmative action.

A. *Affirmative action obligations.* The use of selection procedures which have been validated pursuant to these guidelines does not relieve users of any obligations they may have to undertake affirmative action to assure equal employment opportunity. Nothing in these guidelines is intended to preclude the use of lawful selection procedures which assist in remedying the effects of prior discriminatory practices, or the achievement of affirmative action objectives.

B. *Encouragement of voluntary affirmative action programs.* These guidelines are also intended to encourage the adoption and implementation of voluntary affirmative action programs by users who have no obligation under Federal law to adopt them; but are not intended to impose any new obligations in that regard. The agencies issuing and endorsing these guidelines endorse for all private employers and reaffirm for all governmental employers the Equal Employment Opportunity Coordinating Council's "Policy Statement on Affirmative Action Programs for State and Local Government Agencies" (41 FR 38814, September 13, 1976). That policy statement is attached hereto as appendix, section 17.

Technical Standards

§ 1607.14 Technical standards for validity studies.

The following minimum standards, as applicable, should be met in conducting a validity study. Nothing in these guidelines is intended to preclude the development and use of other professionally acceptable techniques with respect to validation of selection procedures. Where it is not technically feasible for a user to conduct a validity study, the user has the obligation otherwise to comply with

29 CFR Ch. XIV (7-1-90 Edition)

these guidelines. See sections 6 and 7 above.

A. *Validity studies should be based on review of information about the job.* Any validity study should be based upon a review of information about the job for which the selection procedure is to be used. The review should include a job analysis except as provided in section 14B(3) below with respect to criterion-related validity. Any method of job analysis may be used if it provides the information required for the specific validation strategy used.

B. *Technical standards for criterion-related validity studies.* (1) *Technical feasibility.* Users choosing to validate a selection procedure by a criterion-related validity strategy should determine whether it is technically feasible (as defined in section 16) to conduct such a study in the particular employment context. The determination of the number of persons necessary to permit the conduct of a meaningful criterion-related study should be made by the user on the basis of all relevant information concerning the selection procedure, the potential sample and the employment situation. Where appropriate, jobs with substantially the same major work behaviors may be grouped together for validity studies, in order to obtain an adequate sample. These guidelines do not require a user to hire or promote persons for the purpose of making it possible to conduct a criterion-related study.

(2) *Analysis of the job.* There should be a review of job information to determine measures of work behavior(s) or performance that are relevant to the job or group of jobs in question. These measures or criteria are relevant to the extent that they represent critical or important job duties, work behaviors or work outcomes as developed from the review of job information. The possibility of bias should be considered both in selection of the criterion measures and their application. In view of the possibility of bias in subjective evaluations, supervisory rating techniques and instructions to raters should be carefully developed. All criterion measures and the methods for gathering data need to be examined for freedom from factors

Equal Employment Opportunity Comm. § 1607.14

which would unfairly alter scores of members of any group. The relevance of criteria and their freedom from bias are of particular concern when there are significant differences in measures of job performance for different groups.

(3) *Criterion measures.* Proper safeguards should be taken to insure that scores on selection procedures do not enter into any judgments of employee adequacy that are to be used as criterion measures. Whatever criteria are used should represent important or critical work behavior(s) or work outcomes. Certain criteria may be used without a full job analysis if the user can show the importance of the criteria to the particular employment context. These criteria include but are not limited to production rate, error rate, tardiness, absenteeism, and length of service. A standardized rating of overall work performance may be used where a study of the job shows that it is an appropriate criterion. Where performance in training is used as a criterion, success in training should be properly measured and the relevance of the training should be shown either through a comparsion of the content of the training program with the critical or important work behavior(s) of the job(s), or through a demonstration of the relationship between measures of performance in training and measures of job performance. Measures of relative success in training include but are not limited to instructor evaluations, performance samples, or tests. Criterion measures consisting of paper and pencil tests will be closely reviewed for job relevance.

(4) *Representativeness of the sample.* Whether the study is predictive or concurrent, the sample subjects should insofar as feasible be representative of the candidates normally available in the relevant labor market for the job or group of jobs in question, and should insofar as feasible include the races, sexes, and ethnic groups normally available in the relevant job market. In determining the representativeness of the sample in a concurrent validity study, the user should take into account the extent to which the specific knowledges or skills which are the primary focus of the test are

those which employees learn on the job.

Where samples are combined or compared, attention should be given to see that such samples are comparable in terms of the actual job they perform, the length of time on the job where time on the job is likely to affect performance, and other relevant factors likely to affect validity differences; or that these factors are included in the design of the study and their effects identified.

(5) *Statistical relationships.* The degree of relationship between selection procedure scores and criterion measures should be examined and computed, using professionally acceptable statistical procedures. Generally, a selection procedure is considered related to the criterion, for the purposes of these guidelines, when the relationship between performance on the procedure and performance on the criterion measure is statistically significant at the 0.05 level of significance, which means that it is sufficiently high as to have a probability of no more than one (1) in twenty (20) to have occurred by chance. Absence of a statistically significant relationship between a selection procedure and job performance should not necessarily discourage other investigations of the validity of that selection procedure.

(6) *Operational use of selection procedures.* Users should evaluate each selection procedure to assure that it is appropriate for operational use, including establishment of cutoff scores or rank ordering. Generally, if other factors reman the same, the greater the magnitude of the relationship (e.g., correlation coefficent) between performance on a selection procedure and one or more criteria of performance on the job, and the greater the importance and number of aspects of job performance covered by the criteria, the more likely it is that the procedure will be appropriate for use. Reliance upon a selection procedure which is significantly related to a criterion measure, but which is based upon a study involving a large number of subjects and has a low correlation coefficient will be subject to close review if it has a large adverse impact. Sole reliance upon a single selection

instrument which is related to only one of many job duties or aspects of job performance will also be subject to close review. The appropriateness of a selection procedure is best evaluated in each particular situation and there are no minimum correlation coefficients applicable to all employment situations. In determining whether a selection procedure is appropriate for operational use the following considerations should also be taken into account: The degree of adverse impact of the procedure, the availability of other selection procedures of greater or substantially equal validity.

(7) *Overstatement of validity findings.* Users should avoid reliance upon techniques which tend to overestimate validity findings as a result of capitalization on chance unless an appropriate safeguard is taken. Reliance upon a few selection procedures or criteria of successful job performance when many selection procedures or criteria of performance have been studied, or the use of optimal statistical weights for selection procedures computed in one sample, are techniques which tend to inflate validity estimates as a result of chance. Use of a large sample is one safeguard: cross-validation is another.

(8) *Fairness.* This section generally calls for studies of unfairness where technically feasible. The concept of fairness or unfairness of selection procedures is a developing concept. In addition, fairness studies generally require substantial numbers of employees in the job or group of jobs being studied. For these reasons, the Federal enforcement agencies recognize that the obligation to conduct studies of fairness imposed by the guidelines generally will be upon users or groups of users with a large number of persons in a a job class, or test developers; and that small users utilizing their own selection procedures will generally not be obligated to conduct such studies because it will be technically infeasible for them to do so.

(a) *Unfairness defined.* When members of one race, sex, or ethnic group characteristically obtain lower scores on a selection procedure than members of another group, and the differences in scores are not reflected in differences in a measure of job perform-

ance, use of the selection procedure may unfairly deny opportunities to members of the group that obtains the lower scores.

(b) *Investigation of fairness.* Where a selection procedure results in an adverse impact on a race, sex, or ethnic group identified in accordance with the classifications set forth in section 4 above and that group is a significant factor in the relevant labor market, the user generally should investigate the possible existence of unfairness for that group if it is technically feasible to do so. The greater the severity of the adverse impact on a group, the greater the need to investigate the possible existence of unfairness. Where the weight of evidence from other studies shows that the selection procedure predicts fairly for the group in question and for the same or similar jobs, such evidence may be relied on in connection with the selection procedure at issue.

(c) *General considerations in fairness investigations.* Users conducting a study of fairness should review the A.P.A. Standards regarding investigation of possible bias in testing. An investigation of fairness of a selection procedure depends on both evidence of validity and the manner in which the selection procedure is to be used in a particular employment context. Fairness of a selection procedure cannot necessarily be specified in advance without investigating these factors. Investigation of fairness of a selection procedure in samples where the range of scores on selection procedures or criterion measures is severely restricted for any subgroup sample (as compared to other subgroup samples) may produce misleading evidence of unfairness. That factor should accordingly be taken into account in conducting such studies and before reliance is placed on the results.

(d) *When unfairness is shown.* If unfairness is demonstrated through a showing that members of a particular group perform better or poorer on the job than their scores on the selection procedure would indicate through comparison with how members of other groups perform, the user may either revise or replace the selection instrument in accordance with these guidelines, or may continue to use the selection instrument operationally with appropriate revisions in its use to assure compatibility between the probability of successful job performance and the probability of being selected.

(e) *Technical feasibility of fairness studies.* In addition to the general conditions needed for technical feasibility for the conduct of a criterion-related study (see section 16, below) an investigation of fairness requires the following:

(i) An adequate sample of persons in each group available for the study to achieve findings of statistical significance. Guidelines do not require a user to hire or promote persons on the basis of group classifications for the purpose of making it possible to conduct a study of fairness; but the user has the obligation otherwise to comply with these guidelines.

(ii) The samples for each group should be comparable in terms of the actual job they perform, length of time on the job where time on the job is likely to affect performance, and other relevant factors likely to affect validity differences; or such factors should be included in the design of the study and their effects identified.

(f) *Continued use of selection procedures when fairness studies not feasible.* If a study of fairness should otherwise be performed, but is not technically feasible, a selection procedure may be used which has otherwise met the validity standards of these guidelines, unless the technical infeasibility resulted from discriminatory employment practices which are demonstrated by facts other than past failure to conform with requirements for validation of selection procedures. However, when it becomes technically feasible for the user to perform a study of fairness and such a study is otherwise called for, the user should conduct the study of fairness.

C. *Technical standards for content validity studies*—(1) *Appropriateness of content validity studies.* Users choosing to validate a selection procedure by a content validity strategy should determine whether it is appropriate to conduct such a study in the particular employment context. A selection procedure can be supported by a content validity strategy to the extent that it is a representative sample of the content of the job. Selection procedures which purport to measure knowledges, skills, or abilities may in certain circumstances be justified by content validity, although they may not be representative samples, if the knowledge, skill, or ability measured by the selection procedure can be operationally defined as provided in section 14C(4) below, and if that knowledge, skill, or ability is a necessary prerequisite to successful job performance.

A selection procedure based upon inferences about mental processes cannot be supported solely or primarily on the basis of content validity. Thus, a content strategy is not appropriate for demonstrating the validity of selection procedures which purport to measure traits or constructs, such as intelligence, aptitude, personality, commonsense, judgment, leadership, and spatial ability. Content validity is also not an appropriate strategy when the selection procedure involves knowledges, skills, or abilities which an employee will be expected to learn on the job.

(2) *Job analysis for content validity.* There should be a job analysis which includes an analysis of the important work behavior(s) required for successful performance and their relative importance and, if the behavior results in work product(s), an analysis of the work product(s). Any job analysis should focus on the work behavior(s) and the tasks associated with them. If work behavior(s) are not observable, the job analysis should identify and analyze those aspects of the behavior(s) that can be observed and the observed work products. The work behavior(s) selected for measurement should be critical work behavior(s) and/or important work behavior(s) constituting most of the job.

(3) *Development of selection procedures.* A selection procedure designed to measure the work behavior may be developed specifically from the job and job analysis in question, or may have been previously developed by the user, or by other users or by a test publisher.

(4) *Standards for demonstrating content validity.* To demonstrate the content validity of a selection procedure, a user should show that the behavior(s) demonstrated in the selection procedure are a representative sample of the behavior(s) of the job in question or that the selection procedure provides a representative sample of the work product of the job. In the case of a selection procedure measuring a knowledge, skill, or ability, the knowledge, skill, or ability being measured should be operationally defined. In the case of a selection procedure measuring a knowledge, the knowledge being measured should be operationally defined as that body of learned information which is used in and is a necessary prerequisite for observable aspects of work behavior of the job. In the case of skills or abilities, the skill or ability being measured should be operationally defined in terms of observable aspects of work behavior of the job. For any selection procedure measuring a knowledge, skill, or ability the user should show that (a) the selection procedure measures and is a representative sample of that knowledge, skill, or ability; and (b) that knowledge, skill, or ability is used in and is a necessary prerequisite to performance of critical or important work behavior(s). In addition, to be content valid, a selection procedure measuring a skill or ability should either closely approximate an observable work behavior, or its product should closely approximate an observable work product. If a test purports to sample a work behavior or to provide a sample of a work product, the manner and setting of the selection procedure and its level and complexity should closely approximate the work situation. The closer the content and the context of the selection procedure are to work samples or work behaviors, the stronger is the basis for showing content validity. As the content of the selection procedure less resembles a work behavior, or the setting and manner of the administration of the selection procedure less resemble the work situation, or the result less resembles a work product, the less likely the selection procedure is to be content valid,

and the greater the need for other evidence of validity.

(5) *Reliability.* The reliability of selection procedures justified on the basis of content validity should be a matter of concern to the user. Whenever it is feasible, appropriate statistical estimates should be made of the reliability of the selection procedure.

(6) *Prior training or experience.* A requirement for or evaluation of specific prior training or experience based on content validity, including a specification of level or amount of training or experience, should be justified on the basis of the relationship between the content of the training or experience and the content of the job for which the training or experience is to be required or evaluated. The critical consideration is the resemblance between the specific behaviors, products, knowledges, skills, or abilities in the experience or training and the specific behaviors, products, knowledges, skills, or abilities required on the job, whether or not there is close resemblance between the experience or training as a whole and the job as a whole.

(7) *Content validity of training success.* Where a measure of success in a training program is used as a selection procedure and the content of a training program is justified on the basis of content validity, the use should be justified on the relationship between the content of the training program and the content of the job.

(8) *Operational use.* A selection procedure which is supported on the basis of content validity may be used for a job if it represents a critical work behavior (i.e., a behavior which is necessary for performance of the job) or work behaviors which constitute most of the important parts of the job.

(9) *Ranking based on content validity studies.* If a user can show, by a job analysis or otherwise, that a higher score on a content valid selection procedure is likely to result in better job performance, the results may be used to rank persons who score above minimum levels. Where a selection procedure supported solely or primarily by content validity is used to rank job candidates, the selection procedure should measure those aspects of per-

Equal Employment Opportunity Comm. §1607.14

formance which differentiate among levels of job performance.

D. *Technical standards for construct validity studies—* (1) *Appropriateness of construct validity studies.* Construct validity is a more complex strategy than either criterion-related or content validity. Construct validation is a relatively new and developing procedure in the employment field, and there is at present a lack of substantial literature extending the concept to employment practices. The user should be aware that the effort to obtain sufficient empirical support for construct validity is both an extensive and arduous effort involving a series of research studies, which include criterion related validity studies and which may include content validity studies. Users choosing to justify use of a selection procedure by this strategy should therefore take particular care to assure that the validity study meets the standards set forth below.

(2) *Job analysis for construct validity studies.* There should be a job analysis. This job analysis should show the work behavior(s) required for successful performance of the job, or the groups of jobs being studied, the critical or important work behavior(s) in the job or group of jobs being studied, and an identification of the construct(s) believed to underlie successful performance of these critical or important work behaviors in the job or jobs in question. Each construct should be named and defined, so as to distinguish it from other constructs. If a group of jobs is being studied the jobs should have in common one or more critical or important work behaviors at a comparable level of complexity.

(3) *Relationship to the job.* A selection procedure should then be identified or developed which measures the construct identified in accord with subparagraph (2) above. The user should show by empirical evidence that the selection procedure is validly related to the construct and that the construct is validly related to the performance of critical or important work behavior(s). The relationship between the construct as measured by the selection procedure and the related work behavior(s) should be supported by empirical evidence from one or more criterion-related studies involving the job or jobs in question which satisfy the provisions of section 14B above.

(4) *Use of construct validity study without new criterion-related evidence—*(a) *Standards for use.* Until such time as professional literature provides more guidance on the use of construct validity in employment situations, the Federal agencies will accept a claim of construct validity without a criterion-related study which satisfies section 14B above only when the selection procedure has been used elsewhere in a situation in which a criterion-related study has been conducted and the use of a criterion-related validity study in this context meets the standards for transportability of criterion-related validity studies as set forth above in section 7. However, if a study pertains to a number of jobs having common critical or important work behaviors at a comparable level of complexity, and the evidence satisfies subparagraphs 14B (2) and (3) above for those jobs with criterion-related validity evidence for those jobs, the selection procedure may be used for all the jobs to which the study pertains. If construct validity is to be generalized to other jobs or groups of jobs not in the group studied, the Federal enforcement agencies will expect at a minimum additional empirical research evidence meeting the standards of subparagraphs section 14B (2) and (3) above for the additional jobs or groups of jobs.

(b) *Determination of common work behaviors.* In determining whether two or more jobs have one or more work behavior(s) in common, the user should compare the observed work behavior(s) in each of the jobs and should compare the observed work product(s) in each of the jobs. If neither the observed work behavior(s) in each of the jobs nor the observed work product(s) in each of the jobs are the same, the Federal enforcement agencies will presume that the work behavior(s) in each job are different. If the work behaviors are not observable, then evidence of similarity of work products and any other relevant research evidence will be considered in determining whether the work behavior(s) in the two jobs are the same.

DOCUMENTATION OF IMPACT AND VALIDITY EVIDENCE

§ 1607.15 Documentation of impact and validity evidence.

A. *Required information.* Users of selection procedures other than those users complying with section 15A(1) below should maintain and have available for each job information on adverse impact of the selection process for that job and, where it is determined a selection process has an adverse impact, evidence of validity as set forth below.

(1) *Simplified recordkeeping for users with less than 100 employees.* In order to minimize recordkeeping burdens on employers who employ one hundred (100) or fewer employees, and other users not required to file EEO-1, et seq., reports, such users may satisfy the requirements of this section 15 if they maintain and have available records showing, for each year:

(a) The number of persons hired, promoted, and terminated for each job, by sex, and where appropriate by race and national origin;

(b) The number of applicants for hire and promotion by sex and where appropriate by race and national origin; and

(c) The selection procedures utilized (either standardized or not standardized).

These records should be maintained for each race or national origin group (see section 4 above) constituting more than two percent (2%) of the labor force in the relevant labor area. However, it is not necessary to maintain records by race and/or national origin (see § 4 above) if one race or national origin group in the relevant labor area constitutes more than ninety-eight percent (98%) of the labor force in the area. If the user has reason to believe that a selection procedure has an adverse impact, the user should maintain any available evidence of validity for that procedure (see sections 7A and 8).

(2) *Information on impact—(a) Collection of information on impact.* Users of selection procedures other than those complying with section

15A(1) above should maintain and have available for each job records or other information showing whether the total selection process for that job has an adverse impact on any of the groups for which records are called for by sections 4B above. Adverse impact determinations should be made at least annually for each such group which constitutes at least 2 percent of the labor force in the relevant labor area or 2 percent of the applicable workforce. Where a total selection process for a job has an adverse impact, the user should maintain and have available records or other information showing which components have an adverse impact. Where the total selection process for a job does not have an adverse impact, information need not be maintained for individual components except in circumstances set forth in subsection 15A(2)(b) below. If the determination of adverse impact is made using a procedure other than the "four-fifths rule," as defined in the first sentence of section 4D above, a justification, consistent with section 4D above, for the procedure used to determine adverse impact should be available.

(b) *When adverse impact has been eliminated in the total selection process.* Whenever the total selection process for a particular job has had an adverse impact, as defined in section 4 above, in any year, but no longer has an adverse impact, the user should maintain and have available the information on individual components of the selection process required in the preceding paragraph for the period in which there was adverse impact. In addition, the user should continue to collect such information for at least two (2) years after the adverse impact has been eliminated.

(c) *When data insufficient to determine impact.* Where there has been an insufficient number of selections to determine whether there is an adverse impact of the total selection process for a particular job, the user should continue to collect, maintain and have available the information on individual components of the selection process required in section 15(A)(2)(a) above until the information is sufficient to determine that the overall selection process does not have an adverse impact as defined in section 4 above, or until the job has changed substantially.

(3) *Documentation of validity evidence.*—(a) *Types of evidence.* Where a total selection process has an adverse impact (see section 4 above) the user should maintain and have available for each component of that process which has an adverse impact, one or more of the following types of documentation evidence:

(i) Documentation evidence showing criterion-related validity of the selection procedure (see section 15B, below).

(ii) Documentation evidence showing content validity of the selection procedure (see section 15C, below).

(iii) Documentation evidence showing construct validity of the selection procedure (see section 15D, below).

(iv) Documentation evidence from other studies showing validity of the selection procedure in the user's facility (see section 15E, below).

(v) Documentation evidence showing why a validity study cannot or need not be performed and why continued use of the procedure is consistent with Federal law.

(b) *Form of report.* This evidence should be compiled in a reasonably complete and organized manner to permit direct evaluation of the validity of the selection procedure. Previously written employer or consultant reports of validity, or reports describing validity studies completed before the issuance of these guidelines are acceptable if they are complete in regard to the documentation requirements contained in this section, or if they satisfied requirements of guidelines which were in effect when the validity study was completed. If they are not complete, the required additional documentation should be appended. If necessary information is not available the report of the validity study may still be used as documentation, but its adequacy will be evaluated in terms of compliance with the requirements of these guidelines.

(c) *Completeness.* In the event that evidence of validity is reviewed by an enforcement agency, the validation reports completed after the effective date of these guidelines are expected to contain the information set forth below. Evidence denoted by use of the word "(Essential)" is considered critical. If information denoted essential is not included, the report will be considered incomplete unless the user affirmatively demonstrates either its unavailability due to circumstances beyond the user's control or special circumstances of the user's study which make the information irrelevant. Evidence not so denoted is desirable but its absence will not be a basis for considering a report incomplete. The user should maintain and have available the information called for under the heading "Source Data" in sections 15B(11) and 15D(11). While it is a necessary part of the study, it need not be submitted with the report. All statistical results should be organized and presented in tabular or graphic form to the extent feasible.

B. *Criterion-related validity studies.* Reports of criterion-related validity for a selection procedure should include the following information:

(1) *User(s), location(s), and date(s) of study.* Dates and location(s) of the job analysis or review of job information, the date(s) and location(s) of the administration of the selection procedures and collection of criterion data, and the time between collection of data on selection procedures and criterion measures should be provided (Essential). If the study was conducted at several locations, the address of each location, including city and State, should be shown.

(2) *Problem and setting.* An explicit definition of the purpose(s) of the study and the circumstances in which the study was conducted should be provided. A description of existing selection procedures and cutoff scores, if any, should be provided.

(3) *Job anlysis or review of job information.* A description of the procedure used to analyze the job or group of jobs, or to review the job information should be provided (Essential). Where a review of job information results in criteria which may be used without a full job analysis (see section 14B(3)), the basis for the selection of these criteria should be reported (Essential). Where a job analysis is re-

quired a complete description of the work behavior(s) or work outcome(s), and measures of their criticality or importance should be provided (Essential). The report should describe the basis on which the behavior(s) or outcome(s) were determined to be critical or important, such as the proportion of time spent on the respective behaviors, their level of difficulty, their frequency of performance, the consequences of error, or other appropriate factors (Essential). Where two or more jobs are grouped for a validity study, the information called for in this subsection should be provided for each of the jobs, and the justification for the grouping (see section 14B(1)) should be provided (Essential).

(4) *Job titles and codes.* It is desirable to provide the user's job title(s) for the job(s) in question and the corresponding job title(s) and code(s) from U.S. Employment Service's Dictionary of Occupational Titles.

(5) *Criterion measures.* The bases for the selection of the criterion measures should be provided, together with references to the evidence considered in making the selection of criterion measures (essential). A full description of all criteria on which data were collected and means by which they were observed, recorded, evaluated, and quantified, should be provided (essential). If rating techniques are used as criterion measures, the appraisal form(s) and instructions to the rater(s) should be included as part of the validation evidence, or should be explicitly described and available (essential). All steps taken to insure that criterion measures are free from factors which would unfairly alter the scores of members of any group should be described (essential).

(6) *Sample description.* A description of how the research sample was identified and selected should be included (essential). The race, sex, and ethnic composition of the sample, including those groups set forth in section 4A above, should be described (essential). This description should include the size of each subgroup (essential). A description of how the research sample compares with the relevant labor market or work force, the method by which the relevant labor market or work force was defined, and a discussion of the likely effects on validity of differences between the sample and the relevant labor market or work force, are also desirable. Descriptions of educational levels, length of service, and age are also desirable.

(7) *Description of selection procedures.* Any measure, combination of measures, or procedure studied should be completely and explicitly described or attached (essential). If commercially available selection procedures are studied, they should be described by title, form, and publisher (essential). Reports of reliability estimates and how they were established are desirable.

(8) *Techniques and results.* Methods used in analyzing data should be described (essential). Measures of central tendency (e.g., means) and measures of dispersion (e.g., standard deviations and ranges) for all selection procedures and all criteria should be reported for each race, sex, and ethnic group which constitutes a significant factor in the relevant labor market (essential). The magnitude and direction of all relationships between selection procedures and criterion measures investigated should be reported for each relevant race, sex, and ethnic group and for the total group (essential). Where groups are too small to obtain reliable evidence of the magnitude of the relationship, need not be reported separately. Statements regarding the statistical significance of results should be made (essential). Any statistical adjustments, such as for less then perfect reliability or for restriction of score range in the selection procedure or criterion should be described and explained; and uncorrected correlation coefficients should also be shown (essential). Where the statistical technique categorizes continuous data, such as biserial correlation and the phi coefficient, the categories and the bases on which they were determined should be described and explained (essential). Studies of test fairness should be included where called for by the requirements of section 14B(8) (essential). These studies should include the rationale by which a selection procedure was determined to be fair to the group(s) in question. Where test fair-

Equal Employment Opportunity Comm. §1607.15

ness or unfairness has been demonstrated on the basis of other studies, a bibliography of the relevant studies should be included (essential). If the bibliography includes unpublished studies, copies of these studies, or adequate abstracts or summaries, should be attached (essential). Where revisions have been made in a selection procedure to assure compatability between successful job performance and the probability of being selected, the studies underlying such revisions should be included (essential). All statistical results should be organized and presented by relevant race, sex, and ethnic group (essential).

(9) *Alternative procedures investigated.* The selection procedures investigated and available evidence of their impact should be identified (essential). The scope, method, and findings of the investigation, and the conclusions reached in light of the findings, should be fully described (essential).

(10) *Uses and applications.* The methods considered for use of the selection procedure (e.g., as a screening device with a cutoff score, for grouping or ranking, or combined with other procedures in a battery) and available evidence of their impact should be described (essential). This description should include the rationale for choosing the method for operational use, and the evidence of the validity and utility of the procedure as it is to be used (essential). The purpose for which the procedure is to be used (e.g., hiring, transfer, promotion) should be described (essential). If weights are assigned to different parts of the selection procedure, these weights and the validity of the weighted composite should be reported (essential). If the selection procedure is used with a cutoff score, the user should describe the way in which normal expectations of proficiency within the work force were determined and the way in which the cutoff score was determined (essential).

(11) *Source data.* Each user should maintain records showing all pertinent information about individual sample members and raters where they are used, in studies involving the validation of selection procedures. These records should be made available upon request of a compliance agency. In the case of individual sample members these data should include scores on the selection procedure(s), scores on criterion measures, age, sex, race, or ethnic group status, and experience on the specific job on which the validation study was conducted, and may also include such things as education, training, and prior job experience, but should not include names and social security numbers. Records should be maintained which show the ratings given to each sample member by each rater.

(12) *Contact person.* The name, mailing address, and telephone number of the person who may be contacted for further information about the validity study should be provided (essential).

(13) *Accuracy and completeness.* The report should describe the steps taken to assure the accuracy and completeness of the collection, analysis, and report of data and results.

C. *Content validity studies.* Reports of content validity for a selection procedure should include the following information:

(1) *User(s), location(s) and date(s) of study.* Dates and location(s) of the job analysis should be shown (essential).

(2) *Problem and setting.* An explicit definition of the purpose(s) of the study and the circumstances in which the study was conducted should be provided. A description of existing selection procedures and cutoff scores, if any, should be provided.

(3) *Job analysis—Content of the job.* A description of the method used to analyze the job should be provided (essential). The work behavior(s), the associated tasks, and, if the behavior results in a work product, the work products should be completely described (essential). Measures of criticality and/or importance of the work behavior(s) and the method of determining these measures should be provided (essential). Where the job analysis also identified the knowledges, skills, and abilities used in work behavior(s), an operational definition for each knowledge in terms of a body of learned information and for each skill and ability in terms of observable behaviors and outcomes, and the relationship between each knowledge,

skill, or ability and each work behavior, as well as the method used to determine this relationship, should be provided (essential). The work situation should be described, including the setting in which work behavior(s) are performed, and where appropriate, the manner in which knowledges, skills, or abilities are used, and the complexity and difficulty of the knowledge, skill, or ability as used in the work behavior(s).

(4) *Selection procedure and its content.* Selection procedures, including those constructed by or for the user, specific training requirements, composites of selection procedures, and any other procedure supported by content validity, should be completely and explicitly described or attached (essential). If commercially available selection procedures are used, they should be described by title, form, and publisher (essential). The behaviors measured or sampled by the selection procedure should be explicitly described (essential). Where the selection procedure purports to measure a knowledge, skill, or ability, evidence that the selection procedure measures and is a representative sample of the knowledge, skill, or ability should be provided (essential).

(5) *Relationship between the selection procedure and the job.* The evidence demonstrating that the selection procedure is a representative work sample, a representative sample of the work behavior(s), or a representative sample of a knowledge, skill, or ability as used as a part of a work behavior and necessary for that behavior should be provided (essential). The user should identify the work behavior(s) which each item or part of the selection procedure is intended to sample or measure (essential). Where the selection procedure purports to sample a work behavior or to provide a sample of a work product, a comparison should be provided of the manner, setting, and the level of complexity of the selection procedure with those of the work situation (essential). If any steps were taken to reduce adverse impact on a race, sex, or ethnic group in the content of the procedure or in its administration, these steps should be described. Establishment of time

limits, if any, and how these limits are related to the speed with which duties must be performed on the job, should be explained. Measures of central tendency (e.g., means) and measures of dispersion (e.g., standard deviations) and estimates of reliability should be reported for all selection procedures if available. Such reports should be made for relevant race, sex, and ethnic subgroups, at least on a statistically reliable sample basis.

(6) *Alternative procedures investigated.* The alternative selection procedures investigated and available evidence of their impact should be identified (essential). The scope, method, and findings of the investigation, and the conclusions reached in light of the findings, should be fully described (essential).

(7) *Uses and applications.* The methods considered for use of the selection procedure (e.g., as a screening device with a cutoff score, for grouping or ranking, or combined with other procedures in a battery) and available evidence of their impact should be described (essential). This description should include the rationale for choosing the method for operational use, and the evidence of the validity and utility of the procedure as it is to be used (essential). The purpose for which the procedure is to be used (e.g., hiring, transfer, promotion) should be described (essential). If the selection procedure is used with a cutoff score, the user should describe the way in which normal expectations of proficiency within the work force were determined and the way in which the cutoff score was determined (essential). In addition, if the selection procedure is to be used for ranking, the user should specify the evidence showing that a higher score on the selection procedure is likely to result in better job performance.

(8) *Contact person.* The name, mailing address, and telephone number of the person who may be contacted for further information about the validity study should be provided (essential).

(9) *Accuracy and completeness.* The report should describe the steps taken to assure the accuracy and completeness of the collection, analysis, and report of data and results.

D. *Construct validity studies.* Reports of construct validity for a selection procedure should include the following information:

(1) *User(s), location(s), and date(s) of study.* Date(s) and location(s) of the job analysis and the gathering of other evidence called for by these guidelines should be provided (essential).

(2) *Problem and setting.* An explicit definition of the purpose(s) of the study and the circumstances in which the study was conducted should be provided. A description of existing selection procedures and cutoff scores, if any, should be provided.

(3) *Construct definition.* A clear definition of the construct(s) which are believed to underlie successful performance of the critical or important work behavior(s) should be provided (essential). This definition should include the levels of construct performance relevant to the job(s) for which the selection procedure is to be used (essential). There should be a summary of the position of the construct in the psychological literature, or in the absence of such a position, a description of the way in which the definition and measurement of the construct was developed and the psychological theory underlying it (essential). Any quantitative data which identify or define the job constructs, such as factor analyses, should be provided (essential).

(4) *Job analysis.* A description of the method used to analyze the job should be provided (essential). A complete description of the work behavior(s) and, to the extent appropriate, work outcomes and measures of their criticality and/or importance should be provided (essential). The report should also describe the basis on which the behavior(s) or outcomes were determined to be important, such as their level of difficulty, their frequency of performance, the consequences of error or other appropriate factors (essential). Where jobs are grouped or compared for the purposes of generalizing validity evidence, the work behavior(s) and work product(s) for each of the jobs should be described, and conclusions concerning the similarity of the jobs in terms of observable work behaviors or work products should be made (essential).

(5) *Job titles and codes.* It is desirable to provide the selection procedure user's job title(s) for the job(s) in question and the corresponding job title(s) and code(s) from the United States Employment Service's dictionary of occupational titles.

(6) *Selection procedure.* The selection procedure used as a measure of the construct should be completely and explicitly described or attached (essential). If commercially available selection procedures are used, they should be identified by title, form and publisher (essential). The research evidence of the relationship between the selection procedure and the construct, such as factor structure, should be included (essential). Measures of central tendency, variability and reliability of the selection procedure should be provided (essential). Whenever feasible, these measures should be provided separately for each relevant race, sex and ethnic group.

(7) *Relationship to job performance.* The criterion-related study(ies) and other empirical evidence of the relationship between the construct measured by the selection procedure and the related work behavior(s) for the job or jobs in question should be provided (essential). Documentation of the criterion-related study(ies) should satisfy the provisions of section 15B above or section 15E(1) below, except for studies conducted prior to the effective date of these guidelines (essential). Where a study pertains to a group of jobs, and, on the basis of the study, validity is asserted for a job in the group, the observed work behaviors and the observed work products for each of the jobs should be described (essential). Any other evidence used in determining whether the work behavior(s) in each of the jobs is the same should be fully described (essential).

(8) *Alternative procedures investigated.* The alternative selection procedures investigated and available evidence of their impact should be identified (essential). The scope, method, and findings of the investigation, and the conclusions reached in light of the

findings should be fully described (essential).

(9) *Uses and applications.* The methods considered for use of the selection procedure (e.g., as a screening device with a cutoff score, for grouping or ranking, or combined with other procedures in a battery) and available evidence of their impact should be described (essential). This description should include the rationale for choosing the method for operational use, and the evidence of the validity and utility of the procedure as it is to be used (essential). The purpose for which the procedure is to be used (e.g., hiring, transfer, promotion) should be described (essential). If weights are assigned to different parts of the selection procedure, these weights and the validity of the weighted composite should be reported (essential). If the selection procedure is used with a cutoff score, the user should describe the way in which normal expectations of proficiency within the work force were determined and the way in which the cutoff score was determined (essential).

(10) *Accuracy and completeness.* The report should describe the steps taken to assure the accuracy and completeness of the collection, analysis, and report of data and results.

(11) *Source data.* Each user should maintain records showing all pertinent information relating to its study of construct validity.

(12) *Contact person.* The name, mailing address, and telephone number of the individual who may be contacted for further information about the validity study should be provided (essential).

E. *Evidence of validity from other studies.* When validity of a selection procedure is supported by studies not done by the user, the evidence from the original study or studies should be compiled in a manner similar to that required in the appropriate section of this section 15 above. In addition, the following evidence should be supplied:

(1) *Evidence from criterion-related validity studies.*—a. *Job information.* A description of the important job behavior(s) of the user's job and the basis on which the behaviors were determined to be important should be provided (essential). A full description of the basis for determining that these important work behaviors are the same as those of the job in the original study (or studies) should be provided (essential).

b. *Relevance of criteria.* A full description of the basis on which the criteria used in the original studies are determined to be relevant for the user should be provided (essential).

c. *Other variables.* The similarity of important applicant pool or sample characteristics reported in the original studies to those of the user should be described (essential). A description of the comparison between the race, sex and ethnic composition of the user's relevant labor market and the sample in the original validity studies should be provided (essential).

d. *Use of the selection procedure.* A full description should be provided showing that the use to be made of the selection procedure is consistent with the findings of the original validity studies (essential).

e. *Bibliography.* A bibliography of reports of validity of the selection procedure for the job or jobs in question should be provided (essential). Where any of the studies included an investigation of test fairness, the results of this investigation should be provided (essential). Copies of reports published in journals that are not commonly available should be described in detail or attached (essential). Where a user is relying upon unpublished studies, a reasonable effort should be made to obtain these studies. If these unpublished studies are the sole source of validity evidence they should be described in detail or attached (essential). If these studies are not available, the name and address of the source, an adequate abstract or summary of the validity study and data, and a contact person in the source organization should be provided (essential).

(2) *Evidence from content validity studies.* See section 14C(3) and section 15C above.

(3) *Evidence from construct validity studies.* See sections 14D(2) and 15D above.

F. *Evidence of validity from cooperative studies.* Where a selection procedure has been validated through a cooperative study, evidence that the study satisfies the requirements of sections 7, 8 and 15E should be provided (essential).

G. *Selection for higher level job.* If a selection procedure is used to evaluate candidates for jobs at a higher level than those for which they will initially be employed, the validity evidence should satisfy the documentation provisions of this section 15 for the higher level job or jobs, and in addition, the user should provide: (1) a description of the job progression structure, formal or informal; (2) the data showing how many employees progress to the higher level job and the length of time needed to make this progression; and (3) an identification of any anticipated changes in the higher level job. In addition, if the test measures a knowledge, skill or ability, the user should provide evidence that the knowledge, skill or ability is required for the higher level job and the basis for the conclusion that the knowledge, skill or ability is not expected to develop from the training or experience on the job.

H. *Interim use of selection procedures.* If a selection procedure is being used on an interim basis because the procedure is not fully supported by the required evidence of validity, the user should maintain and have available (1) substantial evidence of validity for the procedure, and (2) a report showing the date on which the study to gather the additional evidence commenced, the estimated completion date of the study, and a description of the data to be collected (essential).

(Approved by the Office of Management and Budget under control number 3046-0017)

(Pub. L. No. 96-511, 94 Stat. 2812 (44 U.S.C. 3501 et seq.))

[43 FR 38295, 38312, Aug. 25, 1978, as amended at 46 FR 63268, Dec. 31, 1981]

DEFINITIONS

§1607.16 Definitions.

The following definitions shall apply throughout these guidelines:

A. *Ability.* A present competence to perform an observable behavior or a behavior which results in an observable product.

B. *Adverse impact.* A substantially different rate of selection in hiring, promotion, or other employment decision which works to the disadvantage of members of a race, sex, or ethnic group. See section 4 of these guidelines.

C. *Compliance with these guidelines.* Use of a selection procedure is in compliance with these guidelines if such use has been validated in accord with these guidelines (as defined below), or if such use does not result in adverse impact on any race, sex, or ethnic group (see section 4, above), or, in unusual circumstances, if use of the procedure is otherwise justified in accord with Federal law. See section 6B, above.

D. *Content validity.* Demonstrated by data showing that the content of a selection procedure is representative of important aspects of performance on the job. See section 5B and section 14C.

E. *Construct validity.* Demonstrated by data showing that the selection procedure measures the degree to which candidates have identifiable characteristics which have been determined to be important for successful job performance. See section 5B and section 14D.

F. *Criterion-related validity.* Demonstrated by empirical data showing that the selection procedure is predictive of or significantly correlated with important elements of work behavior. See sections 5B and 14B.

G. *Employer.* Any employer subject to the provisions of the Civil Rights Act of 1964, as amended, including State or local governments and any Federal agency subject to the provisions of section 717 of the Civil Rights Act of 1964, as amended, and any Federal contractor or subcontractor or federally assisted construction contractor or subcontactor covered by Executive Order 11246, as amended.

H. *Employment agency.* Any employment agency subject to the provisions of the Civil Rights Act of 1964, as amended.

I. *Enforcement action.* For the purposes of section 4 a proceeding by a Federal enforcement agency such as a lawsuit or an administrative proceeding leading to debarment from or withholding, suspension, or termination of Federal Government contracts or the suspension or withholding of Federal Government funds; but not a finding of reasonable cause or a conciliation process or the issuance of right to sue letters under title VII or under Executive Order 11246 where such finding, conciliation, or issuance of notice of right to sue is based upon an individual complaint.

J. *Enforcement agency.* Any agency of the executive branch of the Federal Government which adopts these guidelines for purposes of the enforcement of the equal employment opportunity laws or which has responsibility for securing compliance with them.

K. *Job analysis.* A detailed statement of work behaviors and other information relevant to the job.

L. *Job description.* A general statement of job duties and responsibilities.

M. *Knowledge.* A body of information applied directly to the performance of a function.

N. *Labor organization.* Any labor organization subject to the provisions of the Civil Rights Act of 1964, as amended, and any committee subject thereto controlling apprenticeship or other training.

O. *Observable.* Able to be seen, heard, or otherwise perceived by a person other than the person performing the action.

P. *Race, sex, or ethnic group.* Any group of persons identifiable on the grounds of race, color, religion, sex, or national origin.

Q. *Selection procedure.* Any measure, combination of measures, or procedure used as a basis for any employment decision. Selection procedures include the full range of assessment techniques from traditional paper and pencil tests, performance tests, training programs, or probationary periods and physical, educational, and work experience requirements through informal or casual interviews and unscored application forms.

R. *Selection rate.* The proportion of applicants or candidates who are hired, promoted, or otherwise selected.

S. *Should.* The term "should" as used in these guidelines is intended to connote action which is necessary to achieve compliance with the guidelines, while recognizing that there are circumstances where alternative courses of action are open to users.

T. *Skill.* A present, observable competence to perform a learned psychomotor act.

U. *Technical feasibility.* The existence of conditions permitting the conduct of meaningful criterion-related validity studies. These conditions include: (1) An adequate sample of persons available for the study to achieve findings of statistical significance; (2) having or being able to obtain a sufficient range of scores on the selection procedure and job performance measures to produce validity results which can be expected to be representative of the results if the ranges normally expected were utilized; and (3) having or being able to devise unbiased, reliable and relevant measures of job performance or other criteria of employee adequacy. See section 14B(2). With respect to investigation of possible unfairness, the same considerations are applicable to each group for which the study is made. See section 14B(8).

V. *Unfairness of selection procedure.* A condition in which members of one race, sex, or ethnic group characteristically obtain lower scores on a selection procedure than members of another group, and the differences are not reflected in differences in measures of job performance. See section 14B(7).

W. *User.* Any employer, labor organization, employment agency, or licensing or certification board, to the extent it may be covered by Federal equal employment opportunity law, which uses a selection procedure as a basis for any employment decision. Whenever an employer, labor organization, or employment agency is required by law to restrict recruitment for any occupation to those applicants who have met licensing or certification requirements, the licensing or certifying authority to the extent it may be covered by Federal equal employment opportunity law will be considered the user with respect to those licensing or certification requirements. Whenever a State employment agency or service does no more than administer or monitor a procedure as permitted by Department of Labor regulations, and

Equal Employment Opportunity Comm. § 1607.17

does so without making referrals or taking any other action on the basis of the results, the State employment agency will not be deemed to be a user.

X. *Validated in accord with these guidelines or properly validated.* A demonstration that one or more validity study or studies meeting the standards of these guidelines has been conducted, including investigation and, where appropriate, use of suitable alternative selection procedures as contemplated by section 3B, and has produced evidence of validity sufficient to warrant use of the procedure for the intended purpose under the standards of these guidelines.

Y. *Work behavior.* An activity performed to achieve the objectives of the job. Work behaviors involve observable (physical) components and unobservable (mental) components. A work behavior consists of the performance of one or more tasks. Knowledges, skills, and abilities are not behaviors, although they may be applied in work behaviors.

APPENDIX

§ 1607.17 Policy statement on affirmative action (see section 13B).

The Equal Employment Opportunity Coordinating Council was established by act of Congress in 1972, and charged with responsibility for developing and implementing agreements and policies designed, among other things, to eliminate conflict and inconsistency among the agencies of the Federal Government responsible for administering Federal law prohibiting discrimination on grounds of race, color, sex, religion, and national origin. This statement is issued as an initial response to the requests of a number of State and local officials for clarification of the Government's policies concerning the role of affirmative action in the overall equal employment opportunity program. While the Coordinating Council's adoption of this statement expresses only the views of the signatory agencies concerning this important subject, the principles set forth below should serve as policy guidance for other Federal agencies as well.

(1) Equal employment opportunity is the law of the land. In the public sector of our society this means that all persons, regardless of race, color, religion, sex, or national origin shall have equal access to positions in the public service limited only by their ability to do the job. There is ample evidence in all sectors of our society that such equal access frequently has been denied to members of certain groups because of their sex, racial, or ethnic characteristics. The remedy for such past and present discrimination is twofold.

On the one hand, vigorous enforcement of the laws against discrimination is essential. But equally, and perhaps even more important are affirmative, voluntary efforts on the part of public employers to assure that positions in the public service are genuinely and equally accessible to qualified persons, without regard to their sex, racial, or ethnic characteristics. Without such efforts equal employment opportunity is no more than a wish. The importance of voluntary affirmative action on the part of employers is underscored by title VII of the Civil Rights Act of 1964, Executive Order 11246, and related laws and regulations—all of which emphasize voluntary action to achieve equal employment opportunity.

As with most management objectives, a systematic plan based on sound organizational analysis and problem identification is crucial to the accomplishment of affirmative action objectives. For this reason, the Council urges all State and local governments to develop and implement results oriented affirmative action plans which deal with the problems so identified.

The following paragraphs are intended to assist State and local governments by illustrating the kinds of analyses and activities which may be appropriate for a public employer's voluntary affirmative action plan. This statement does not address remedies imposed after a finding of unlawful discrimination.

(2) Voluntary affirmative action to assure equal employment opportunity is appropriate at any stage of the employment process. The first step in the construction of any affirmative action

plan should be an analysis of the employer's work force to determine whether precentages of sex, race, or ethnic groups in individual job classifications are substantially similar to the precentages of those groups available in the relevant job market who possess the basic job-related qualifications.

When substantial disparities are found through such analyses, each element of the overall selection process should be examined to determine which elements operate to exclude persons on the basis of sex, race, or ethnic group. Such elements include, but are not limited to, recruitment, testing, ranking certification, interview, recommendations for selection, hiring, promotion, etc. The examination of each element of the selection process should at a minimum include a determination of its validity in predicting job performance.

(3) When an employer has reason to believe that its selection procedures have the exclusionary effect described in paragraph 2 above, it should initiate affirmative steps to remedy the situation. Such steps, which in design and execution may be race, color, sex, or ethnic "conscious," include, but are not limited to, the following:

(a) The establishment of a long-term goal, and short-range, interim goals and timetables for the specific job classifications, all of which should take into account the availability of basically qualified persons in the relevant job market;

(b) A recruitment program designed to attract qualified members of the group in question;

(c) A systematic effort to organize work and redesign jobs in ways that provide opportunities for persons lacking "journeyman" level knowledge or skills to enter and, with appropriate training, to progress in a career field;

(d) Revamping selection instruments or procedures which have not yet been validated in order to reduce or eliminate exclusionary effects on particular groups in particular job classifications;

(e) The initiation of measures designed to assure that members of the affected group who are qualified to perform the job are included within the pool of persons from which the selecting official makes the selection;

(f) A systematic effort to provide career advancement training, both classroom and on-the-job, to employees locked into dead end jobs; and

(g) The establishment of a system for regularly monitoring the effectiveness of the particular affirmative action program, and procedures for making timely adjustments in this program where effectiveness is not demonstrated.

(4) The goal of any affirmative action plan should be achievement of genuine equal employment opportunity for all qualified persons. Selection under such plans should be based upon the ability of the applicant(s) to do the work. Such plans should not require the selection of the unqualified, or the unneeded, nor should they require the selection of persons on the basis of race, color, sex, religion, or national origin. Moreover, while the Council believes that this statement should serve to assist State and local employers, as well as Federal agencies, it recognizes that affirmative action cannot be viewed as a standardized program which must be accomplished in the same way at all times in all places.

Accordingly, the Council has not attempted to set forth here either the minimum or maximum voluntary steps that employers may take to deal with their respective situations. Rather, the Council recognizes that under applicable authorities, State and local employers have flexibility to formulate affirmative action plans that are best suited to their particular situations. In this manner, the Council believes that affirmative action programs will best serve the goal of equal employment opportunity.

Respectfully submitted,

Harold R. Tyler, Jr.,
Deputy Attorney General and Chairman of the Equal Employment Coordinating Council.

Michael H. Moskow,
Under Secretary of Labor.

Ethel Bent Walsh,
Acting Chairman, Equal Employment Opportunity Commission.

Robert E. Hampton,
Chairman, Civil Service Commission.

Arthur E. Flemming,
Chairman, Commission on Civil Rights.

Because of its equal employment opportunity responsibilities under the State and Local Government Fiscal Assistance Act of 1972 (the revenue sharing act), the Department of Treasury was invited to participate in the formulation of this policy statement; and it concurs and joins in the adoption of this policy statement.

Done this 26th day of August 1976.

Richard Albrecht,
General Counsel,
Department of the Treasury.

§ 1607.18 Citations.

The official title of these guidelines is "Uniform Guidelines on Employee Selection Procedures (1978)". The Uniform Guidelines on Employee Selection Procedures (1978) are intended to establish a uniform Federal position in the area of prohibiting discrimination in employment practices on grounds of race, color, religion, sex, or national origin. These guidelines have been adopted by the Equal Employment Opportunity Commission, the Department of Labor, the Department of Justice, and the Civil Service Commission.

The official citation is:

"Section ——, Uniform Guidelines on Employee Selection Procedure (1978); 43 FR —— (August 25, 1978)."

The short form citation is:

"Section ——, U.G.E.S.P. (1978); 43 FR —— (August 25, 1978)."

When the guidelines are cited in connection with the activities of one of the issuing agencies, a specific citation to the regulations of that agency can be added at the end of the above citation. The specific additional citations are as follows:

Equal Employment Opportunity Commission
29 CFR Part 1607
Department of Labor
Office of Federal Contract Compliance Programs
41 CFR Part 60–3
Department of Justice
28 CFR 50.14
Civil Service Commission
5 CFR 300.103(c)

Normally when citing these guidelines, the section number immediately preceding the title of the guidelines will be from these guidelines series 1–

18. If a section number from the codification for an individual agency is needed it can also be added at the end of the agency citation. For example, section 6A of these guidelines could be cited for EEOC as follows: "Section 6A, Uniform Guidelines on Employee Selection Procedures (1978); 43 FR ——, (August 25, 1978); 29 CFR Part 1607, section 6A."

PART 1608—AFFIRMATIVE ACTION APPROPRIATE UNDER TITLE VII OF THE CIVIL RIGHTS ACT OF 1964, AS AMENDED

Sec.
1608.1 Statement of purpose.
1608.2 Written interpretation and opinion.
1608.3 Circumstances under which voluntary affirmative action is appropriate.
1608.4 Establishing affirmative action plans.
1608.5 Affirmative action compliance programs under Executive Order No. 11246, as amended.
1608.6 Affirmative action plans which are part of Commission conciliation or settlement agreements.
1608.7 Affirmative action plans or programs under State or local law.
1608.8 Adherence to court order.
1608.9 Reliance on directions of other government agencies. -
1608.10 Standard of review.
1608.11 Limitations on the application of these guidelines.
1608.12 Equal employment opportunity plans adopted pursuant to section 717 of Title VII.

AUTHORITY: Sec. 713 the Civil Rights Act of 1964, as amended, 42 U.S.C. 2000e–12, 78 Stat. 265.

SOURCE: 44 FR 4422, Jan. 19, 1979, unless otherwise noted.

§ 1608.1 Statement of purpose.

(a) *Need for Guidelines.* Since the passage of Title VII in 1964, many employers, labor organizations, and other persons subject to Title VII have changed their employment practices and systems to improve employment opportunities for . minorities and women, and this must continue. These changes have been undertaken either on the initiative of the employer, labor organization, or other person subject to Title VII, or as a result of concilia-

APPENDIX B

HIRING POLICY OF THE AKRON-SUMMIT COUNTY PUBLIC LIBRARY

2.00 EMPLOYMENT PRACTICES AND POLICIES

2.01 Employment Practices-General

The Akron-Summit County Public Library is an equal opportunity employer. Discrimination on the basis of age, race, color, religion, sex, national origin, handicap or ancestry with respect to any matter related to employment is strictly prohibited. The Board of Trustees adopted an Affirmative Action Plan on September 1, 1977. Violations of the Affirmative Action Plan or the general library policy against discrimination may result in disciplinary action up to and including termination. If an employee feels that he or she is the object of discrimination on the job, he or she should contact the Personnel Director or Librarian-Director.

2.02 Job Openings

Job openings and employment opportunities in the library are announced in writing to the staff five working days before other applicants are interviewed. The Librarian-Director reserves the prerogative, however, to reassign staff if the Librarian-Director determines that such reassignment is in the best interest of the library.

2.03 Appointments

The selection of individuals to fill positions is made and salaries are set by the Board of Trustees, on the recommendation of the Librarian-Director. Selection is based on the requirements of the position and the educational, technical, professional, intellectual and personal qualifications of the candidates. Among the personal qualifications should be an ability to work well with staff members and the public. The library will not consider an applicant for a position which would place him or her under the direct supervision of an immediate family member, or in a position where he or she would directly supervise a member of the immediate family. (See Section 6.00, "Immediate Family.")

All individuals appointed to positions will be expected to serve for at least one year as employees of the library system. Individuals appointed to full-time regular positions will be expected to serve at least six months in the agency to which they are appointed. All individuals hired by the system or employees appointed to new positions are on probationary status for six months. If, for any reason, the Librarian-Director decides to terminate employment during the probationary period, it may be done with the usual notice given. (See Section 2.05, "Resignations.")

2.03   Appointments (cont.)

Following completion of the probationary period, the employment (but not assignment) of an employee, unless appointed on a temporary basis, carries with it the expectation of continuous and permanent employment as long as the employee performs assigned tasks competently, and conducts himself or herself in accordance with the policies and practices of the library. The Librarian-Director reserves the right to reduce staff or eliminate positions due to financial exigencies, changes in library service, realignment of function, or adoption of new methods.

2.04 Promotions and Transfers

When there are openings, the library evaluates for promotion or transfer interested employees who have the qualifications for the position. The library is also free to seek candidates from sources outside the library in order to fill each position with the best qualified person.

Announcement of a vacancy is always made to employees prior to announcing the position outside the library. Any interested, qualified employee may apply for the vacant position orally or in writing. Application for a support staff position should be made before the specified deadline date to the Personnel Director. Application for professional positions must be made before the deadline date to the Librarian-Director, or the Personnel Director in the absence of the Librarian-Director.

Promotions and transfers are based upon evidence of satisfactory performance as indicated on the performance evaluations, promise of future development, education, experience, technical expertise and personal qualifications. All employees who are promoted or transferred are on probation for six months. If a promoted or transferred employee fails to fulfill the duties and responsibilities of a new position during the probationary period, the employee may be placed in a lower grade position. Newly promoted or transferred full-time employees may not apply for transfer or promotion outside the agency for six months.

Transfers may be initiated by the Librarian-Director when the Librarian-Director feels that such a transfer is in the best interest of the library. Whenever possible, the needs and desires of the employee are taken into consideration. The library will not consider an applicant for a position which would place the applicant under the direct supervision of an immediate family member, or in a position which directly supervises an immediate family member. (See Section 6.00 "Immediate Family".)

APPENDIX C

SAMPLE "AT WILL" STATEMENT

... While this manual sets forth personnel policies and procedures, it is not to be construed or deemed in whole or in part an employment contract or agreement. CAMLS hopes that your employment will be rewarding, but both you and CAMLS reserve the right to terminate our employment relationship for any reason at any time. Nothing contained in this handbook should be considered to alter the at-will relationship between you and CAMLS. Simply put, this means that both you and CAMLS retain the right to end the relationship at any time for any reason. Further, the personnel policies and procedures contained in this handbook, and the terms and conditions of your employment can be modified only by the Board of Trustees of CAMLS. No employee of CAMLS, other than the Executive Director has any authority to enter into any agreement for any specific period of time or to make any promise regarding the terms and conditions of your employment.

FROM *Employee Handbook*, Cleveland Area Metropolitan Library System, Cleveland, Ohio, p.2.

APPENDIX D

Name _____

Pro	SA
LA	O
CT/Sec	GA
M	

Date _____

Akron-Summit County Public Library
Employment Application

In compliance with Federal and State equal employment opportunity laws, qualified applicants are considered for positions without regard to race, color, religion, sex, national origin, age, marital status, or the presence of a non-job related medical condition or disability.

Akron-Summit County Public Library

Identification

Name: Last	First	Middle

Street Address	Telephone Number

City	State	Zip	Social Securtiy No.

Under 18?   Yes _____ No _____   U.S. Citizen or legal alien? Yes _____ No _____

General Information

Are you interested in full time work? _____ Part time work? _____ Job Share? _____

Can you work evenings and weekends? _____

List professional, business, civic or volunteer activities and offices held: (Omit any group which would indicate race, color, religion, sex, national origin or age).

_____

_____

_____

Have you served in the U.S. Military? _____ If so, give dates and branch of service: _____

_____

_____

Have you ever been convicted of a felony? _____ If so, give date of conviction and describe the nature of the offense:

_____

_____

What types of jobs are you interested in?

❑ Professional Librarian ❑ Clerical/Secretarial ❑ Library Assistant ❑ Custodial

❑ Graphic Artist ❑ Technical ❑ Driver ❑ Other, please specify _____

Training	Circle Highest Year Completed	Name and City	Did you Graduate? (circle)	Major Subjects or Types of Courses	Grade Point Average
High School	Years 9 10 11 12		Yes No		
Business Correspondence or Vocational School	No. of Months		Yes No		
College or University	Years 1 2 3 4		Yes No	Degree Received	
Graduate School	Years 1 2 3 4		Yes No	Degree Received	
Other Courses Or Special Training	No. of Months		Yes No		

SPECIAL SKILLS (include knowledge of Audio Visual Equipment, Word Processing, etc.)	Shorthand Speed wpm:
	Typing Speed wpm:

Employment Please start with current position first

Place of Employment	Position
	Duties
Address	Reason for Leaving
Supervisor's Name	Dates of Employment: From_____To_____
May we contact this employer? Yes ❑ No ❑	Rate of Pay

complete form by continuing on back

Employment (continued)

Place of Employment	Position
	Duties
Address	Reason For Leaving
Supervisor's name	Dates of Employment: From_____ To_____
May we contact this employer? Yes ☐ No ☐	Rate of Pay
Place of Employment	Position
	Duties
Address	Reason For Leaving
Supervisor's name	Dates of Employment: From_____ To_____
May we contact this employer? Yes ☐ No ☐	Rate of Pay
Place of Employment	Position
	Duties
Address	Reason For Leaving
Supervisor's name	Dates of Employment: From_____ To_____
May we contact this employer? Yes ☐ No ☐	Rate of Pay

Agreement (please read before signing)

I certify that answers given herein are true and complete to the best of my knowledge.

I authorize you to make such investigations and inquiries of my personal, employment, financial or medical history and other related matters as may be necessary in arriving at an employment decision. I hereby release employers, schools, or persons from liability in responding to inquiries in connection with my application.

In the event of employment, I understand that false or misleading information given on the application or in the interview(s) may result in discharge. I understand, also, that I am required to abide by all rules and regulations of the Akron-Summit County Public Library.

Date _____ **Signature** _____

The Akron-Summit County Public Library is an Equal Opportunity Employer.
#PERS-350 (5-92)

APPLICATION FOR EMPLOYMENT
LEXINGTON PUBLIC LIBRARY
140 East Main Street
Lexington, Kentucky 40507-1376
(606) 231-5500

Please answer all questions as completely as possible. The use of this application does not create a contract between you and the Lexington Public Library, does not indicate that there are positions open and does not in any way obligate you or the Lexington Public Library. The Lexington Public Library does not discriminate in employment on the basis of race, sex, age, handicap, religion, color, national origin, status as a Vietnam Era Veteran, status as a disabled Veteran, or because an individual is a smoker or nonsmoker, as long as such individual complies with any workplace policy concerning smoking.

PLEASE PRINT IN INK OR TYPE

Date _____ | _____ | _____

Name _____

     Last   First   Middle

Social Security Number _____ | _____ | _____

Address _____

     Street   City   State   Zip Code

Phone _____

Position(s) applying for _____ Full-time _____ Part-time _____

Salary requirement _____ Date available to begin work _____

If desiring part-time work, days and hours available _____

Are you legally eligible for employment in the United States? Yes ☐ No ☐
(Proof of U.S. citizenship or immigration status will be required upon employment.)

If you are less than 18 years of age, please give your age _____

Have you been convicted of a felony within the last 7 years? Yes ☐ No ☐
(If you have been convicted it does not automatically mean you will not be hired. What you were convicted of, and how long ago, are important.)

If yes, please state all pertinent information concerning each conviction, including date, place and nature of conviction:

_____

_____

Have your ever been known by any other name(s) which the Lexington Public Library will need to know to verify any of the information contained in this application? Yes ☐ No ☐ If yes, give name(s) and identify the related school, employer, etc.

_____

Have you ever been employed by this Library? Yes ☐ No ☐ If yes, please complete:

Branch/Dept. _____ Employed from _____ to _____

Does the Lexington Public Library **now** employ any of your relatives? Yes ☐ No ☐
    If yes, please state:

Name(s) _____ Dept. _____ Relationship _____

AN EQUAL OPPORTUNITY AFFIRMATIVE ACTION EMPLOYER

EMPLOYMENT RECORD

List your current or most recent employer first and indicate a continuous record of employment for the last five employers or from the time you left school. (Please add a supplementary sheet if additional space is required.)

If currently employed, may your employer be contacte at this time for a reference? Yes ☐ No ☐

Employer	Address	Phone

Employed (Mo/Yr)	Salary Starting	At Termination (or at present)	Name of Supervisor
From To			

Job Title and Duties	Reason for Leaving

Employer	Address	Phone

Employed (Mo/Yr)	Salary Starting	At Termination (or at present)	Name of Supervisor
From To			

Job Title and Duties	Reason for Leaving

Employer	Address	Phone

Employed (Mo/Yr)	Salary Starting	At Termination (or at present)	Name of Supervisor
From To			

Job Title and Duties	Reason for Leaving

Employer	Address	Phone

Employed (Mo/Yr)	Salary Starting	At Termination (or at present)	Name of Supervisor
From To			

Job Title and Duties	Reason for Leaving

Employer	Address	Phone

Employed (Mo/Yr)	Salary Starting	At Termination (or at present)	Name of Supervisor
From To			

Job Title and Duties	Reason for Leaving

EDUCATION

Circle highest grade completed:

	Grade School	High School	College	Graduate School
	1 2 3 4 5 6 7 8	9 10 11 12	1 2 3 4	1 2 3 4

List all schools attended: high school, technical/vocational, college, business, military, etc.
Use another sheet if necessary

School	Did you Graduate?	Certification or Degree Received	Major/Minor Subjects
Name _____	Yes ☐		
Address _____	No ☐		
Name _____	Yes ☐		
Address _____	No ☐		
Name _____	Yes ☐		
Address _____	No ☐		
Name _____	Yes ☐		
Address _____	No ☐		

SPECIALIZED TRAINING SKILLS

List all current licenses and/or areas of certification (if not listed above): _____

_____

List all equipment (office, trade or laboratory) that you operate proficiently: _____

_____

List any other training, skills, aptitudes and qualifications which you feel are relevant to the type of employment you are seeking at

the Library: _____

_____

READ CAREFULLY BEFORE SIGNING

I certify that the information given by me in this application is true and complete. I understand and agree that any false information, misrepresentation, or concealment of fact is sufficient grounds for either my immediate discharge without recourse or refusal of employment by the Lexington Public Library.

I agree that if I am employed by the Lexington Public Library my employment may be terminated at any time without liability except such wages as may have been earned at the date of such termination. I further understand and acknowledge that this is an application for employment, that no employment contract is being offered and that if I am employed such employment is for an indefinite period of time and that the Library can change wages, benefits and conditions at any time.

I understand and agree that all information furnished in this application may be verified by the Lexington Public Library. I also understand that any employment is subject to a satisfactory check of references and a Police Department background check. I hereby authorize all individuals and organizations named or referred to in this application and any law enforcement organization to give the Library all information relative to my employment, work habits, and character and hereby release such individuals, organizations, and the Library from any liability for any claim or damage which may result.

Signature _____ Date _____

Lexington Public Library
140 East Main Street
Lexington, Kentucky 40507-1376
(606) 231-5500

Completion of this form is voluntary. This form will be kept in a file separate from your application.

INVITATION TO VIETNAM ERA VETERANS AND DISABLED VETERANS

The Lexington Public Library ("Library") is a government contractor/grantee subject to section 402 of the Vietnam Era Veterans Readjustment Assistance Act of 1974 which requires government contractors to take affirmative action to employ and advance in employment qualified disabled veterans and veterans of the Vietnam Era. If you are a disabled Veteran covered by this program and would like to be considered under the affirmative action program, please tell us. This information is voluntary and refusal to provide it will not subject you to discharge or disciplinary treatment. Information obtained concerning individuals shall be kept confidential, except that (1) supervisors and managers may be informed regarding restrictions on the work or duties of disabled veterans, and regarding necessary accommodations, and (2) first aid personnel may be informed, when and to the extent appropriate, if the condition might require emergency treatment. In order to assure proper placement of all employees, we do request that you answer the following question: If you have a disability which might affect your performance or create a hazard to yourself or others in connection with the job for which you are applying, please state the following: (1) the skills, procedures, and aids you use or intend to use to perform the job notwithstanding the disability and (2) the accommodations the Library could make which would enable you to perform the job properly and safely, such as special equipment, changes in the physical layout of the job, and/or changes in certain duties relating to the job or other accommodations.

_____

_____

INVITATION TO APPLICANTS FOR EMPLOYMENT TO IDENTIFY THEMSELVES AS HANDICAPPED

THIS SECTION PERTAINS ONLY TO QUALIFIED INDIVIDUALS WITH HANDICAPS. A "qualified individual with handicaps" is any person who has a physical or mental impairment that substantially limits one or more major life activities, has a record of such impairment or is regarded as having such impairment. The Lexington Public Library ("Library") is subject to section 504 of the Vocational Rehabilitation Act of 1973 which requires certain employers to take affirmative action to employ qualified individuals with handicaps. If you feel you meet the above definition of "qualified individual with handicap," the Library invites you to inform us so that you may be given consideration under the Library's affirmative action program.

Provision of this information is entirely voluntary, and failure to provide it will not result in any adverse treatment. The information will be used only in accordance with section 504 of the Vocational Rehabilitation Act of 1973. The information provided will be kept confidential, except that (1) supervisors or other employees may be informed regarding restrictions on the work or duties of qualified individuals with handicaps and any necessary reasonable accommodations; and (2) first aid personnel may be informed, where appropriate, if the condition might require emergency treatment; and (3) government officials investigating compliance with the Act shall be informed.

Please describe handicap: _____

If you have a handicap which might affect your performance or create a hazard to yourself or others in connection with the job for which you are applying, please indicate below (1) the skills, procedures, and aids you use or intend to use to perform the job, and (2) the accommodations the Library could make which would enable you to perform the job properly and safely, such as special equipment, changes in the physical layout of the job, and/or changes in certain duties of the job.

_____

_____

_____   _____
Signature   Date

_____   _____
PRINT FULL NAME   SS#

Rev. 12/90

APPENDIX E

Questions That Should Not be Asked in an Interview

AREA OF INQUIRY	LEGAL	ILLEGAL
1. Name	a) For access purposes, inquiry into whether the applicant's work records are under another name.	a) To ask if a woman is a Miss, Mrs. or Ms. b) To request applicant to give maiden name, or any other previous name her or she has used.
2. Address/Housing	a) To request place and length of current and previous addresses. b) To ask for applicant's phone number or how he or she can be reached.	
3. Age	a) Require proof of age by birth certificate, *after hiring*.	a) To ask age or age group of applicant. b) To request birth certificate or baptismal record before hiring.
4. Birthplace/National Origin		a) To ask birthplace of applicant or that of his or her parents, grandparents or spouse. b) Any other inquiry into national origin.
5. Race/Color	a) To indicate that the institution is an equal opportunity employer. b) To ask race for affirmative action plan statistics, *after hiring*.	a) Any inquiry that would indicate race or color.
6. Sex	a) To indicate that the institution is an equal opportunity employer. b) To ask sex for affirmative action plan statistics, *after hiring*.	a) To ask applicant any inquiry which would indicate sex, unless job-related (Only such jobs in education would be a full-time locker room or restroom attendant.)
7. Religion/Creed		a) To ask an applicant's religion or religious customs and holidays. b) To request recommendations from church officials.
8. Citizenship	a) Whether a U.S. citizen. b) If not, whether intends to become one. c) If U.S. residence is legal. d) If spouse is a citizen. e) Require proof of citizenship, *after hiring*	a) If native-born or naturalized. b) Proof of citizenship before hiring. c) Whether parents or spouse is native-born or naturalized. d) Date of citizenship.
9. Marital/Parental Status	a) Status (only married or single) *after hiring* for insurance and tax purposes. b) Number and ages of dependents and age of spouse *after hiring* for insurance and tax purposes.	a) To ask marital status *before hiring*. b) To ask the number and age of children, who cares for them and if applicant plans to have more children.
10. Relatives	a) To ask name, relationship and address of person to be notified in case of emergency, *after hiring*.	a) Names of relatives working for the institution or in a district (nepotism policies which impact disparately on one sex are illegal under Title IX.)
11. Military Service	a) Inquiry into service in the U.S. armed forces. b) Branch of service and rank attained. c) Any job-related experience. d) Require military discharge certificate *after hiring*.	a) To request military service records. b) To ask about military service in armed service of any country other than the U.S. c) Type of discharge.

AREA OF INQUIRY	LEGAL	ILLEGAL
12. Education	a) To ask what academic, professional or vocational schools attended. b) To ask about language skills, such as reading and writing foreign languages.	a) Specifically ask the nationality, racial or religious affiliation of schools attended. b) To ask how foreign language ability was acquired.
13. Criminal Record	a) To request listing of convictions other than misdemeanors.	a) To inquire about arrests.
14. References	a) To request general and work references not relating to race, color, religion, sex, national origin or ancestry.	a) To request references specifically from clergy or any other persons who might reflect race, color, religion, sex, national origin or ancestry.
15. Organizations	a) To ask organizational membership—professional, social, etc.—so long as affiliation is not used to discriminate on the basis of race, sex, national origin or ancestry. b) Offices held, if any.	a) To request listing of *all* clubs applicant belongs to or has belonged to.
16. Photographs	a) May be required *after hiring* for identification purposes.	a) Request photographs before hiring. b) To take pictures of applicants during interview.
17. Work Schedule	a) To ask willingness to work required work schedule. b) To ask if applicant has military reservist obligations.	a) To ask willingness to work any particular religious holiday.
18. Physical Data	a) To require applicant to prove ability to do manual labor, lifting and other physical requirements of the job, if any. b) Require a physical examination.	a) To ask height and weight, impairment or other non-specified job-related physical data.
19. Disability	a) No inquiries unless applicant volunteers that they have a disability. Even then questions should be focussed on reasonable accommodations.	a) To ask questions about an individual's disability or to exclude disabled applicants as a class on the basis of their disability.
20. Other qualifications	a) To inquire about any area that has a direct reflection on the job applied for.	a) Any non-job related inquiry that may present information permitting unlawful discrimination.

APPENDIX F

TELEPHONE REFERENCE FORM

Date and time of call _____ Date(s) of unsuccesful attempts _____

Name of candidate _____

Name of referree _____ Position _____

Relationship of
candidate to referee _____

Dates of employment From _____ To _____

What were the candidate's primary responsibilities? _____

_____

Was the candidate a good performer? _____

_____

What were the candidate's strengths? _____

_____

What were the candidate's weaknesses? _____

_____

Was the candidate reliable in meeting a regular work schedule? _____

_____

Did the candidate get along well with co-workers? _____

_____

Did the candidate get along well with members of the public? _____

_____

Why did the employee leave this position? _____

_____

Would you rehire this individual? _____

_____

Name of reference checker _____

Others present during check _____

APPENDIX G

SAMPLE LETTER OF APPOINTMENT

Dear _____ :

This letter is to confirm our offer for a full-time appointment as a Librarian II at the Smithly Public Library. This appointment is subject to the final approval of the Board of Trustees. All newly hired employees are on probationary status for six months from the date of employment.

Your starting assignment is in the Reference Department of the Main library, and your supervisor is Janice Morgan. Your salary is $23,500 per year and your starting date is June 13, 1993. Please report to her at the Reference Department at 9:00am on June 13th. At that time, she will begin your orientation and training.

Congratulations on your appointment! I hope that you find your employment with our library to be an enjoyable and rewarding experience.

Sincerely yours,

Suzanne Oglethorpe
Personnel Director

APPENDIX H

ORIENTATION CHECKLIST

1. Terms of employment: probationary/temporary status   ————
2. Work scheduling including work week, breaks, how to report in sick   ————
3. Types of leaves: sick leave, vacation, holidays etc.   ————
4. Number of vacation and sick days and how they are earned   ————
5. Insurance benefits: ————

> Hospitalization/HMO
> Dental
> Life

6. Retirement system   ————
7. Pay period and rate, overtime, and how pay is received   ————
8. Counselling services   ————
9. Other benefits: ————

> Annuities/Tax sheltered plans
> Savings plans

10. Performance evaluation policy   ————
11. Discipline policy/grievance procedures   ————
12. Job description reviewed   ————
13. Opportunities for advancement   ————
14. History and purpose of the library   ————
15. Tour of the building   ————

The above information has been explained to me and I have received a copy of the *Staff Handbook*.

Employee _____ Date _____

Personnel representative _____ Date _____

BIBLIOGRAPHY

GENERAL AND LIBRARY-RELATED WORKS ON PERSONNEL MANAGEMENT

Creth Sheila and Frederick Duda. *Personnel Administration in Libraries*. New York, Neal-Schuman, 1989.

Jones, Noragh and Peter Jordan. *Staff Management in Library and Information Work*, 2nd edition. Aldershot Hants, England: Gower Publishing, 1987.

Kahn, Steven C., Barbara A. Brown, and Brent E. Zepke. *Personnel Directors Legal Guide*, 2nd edition. Boston: Warren, Gorham and Lamont, 1990.

Rubin, Richard. *Human Resource Management in Libraries*. New York: Neal-Schuman, 1991.

Rubin, Richard, Ed. *Personnel Management in Libraries*, special issue of *Library Trends* 38 (Summer 1989).

Stueart, Robert and Barbara Moran. *Library Management*, 3rd Edition. Littleton, CO: Libraries Unlimited, 1987.

White, Herbert S. *Library Personnel Management*. White Plains: Knowledge Industry Publications, 1985.

GENERAL AND LIBRARY-RELATED WORKS ON HIRING

Byham, William C. "Screening and Selection," In *Human Resources Management and Development Handbook*, New York: AMACOM, 1985, 520-574.

Fear, James A. and James F. Ross. *Jobs, Dollars, and EEO: How to Hire More Productive Entry-Level Workers.* New York: McGraw-Hill, 1983.

Feild, Hubert S. and Robert D. Gatewood, "Matching Talent with the Task," *Personnel Administrator* (April 1987): 113-126.

Fernandez, Linda. *Now Hiring: An Employer's Guide to Recruiting in a Tight Labor Market.* Washington, D.C.: BNA, 1989.

Ferris, Gerald R. *Organizational Entry.* Greenwich, CT.: JAI, 1990. (Research oriented)

Isacco, Jeanne M. and Catherine Smith. "Hiring: A Common Sense Approach," *Journal of Library Administration* 6 (Summer 1985): 67-81.

WORKS ON INTERVIEWING

Creth, Sheila. "Conducting an Effective Employment Interview," *Journal of Academic Librarianship* 4 (November 1978): 356-360.

Drake, John D. *Interviewing for Managers: A Complete Guide to Employment Interviewing.* New York: AMACOM, 1982.

Hatfield, John D. and Robert D. Gatewood. "Nonverbal Cues in the Selection Interview," *Personnel Administrator* 23 (January 1978): 30, 35-37.

Lopez, Felix M. *Personnel Interviewing: Theory and Practice,* X ed., New York: McGraw-Hill, 1975.

Loretto, Vincent. "Effective Interviewing Is Based on More Than Intuition," *Personnel Journal* 65 (December 1986): 101-107.

Peele, David. "Fear in the Library," *Journal of Academic Librarianship* 4 (November 1978): 361-365.

RESEARCH ORIENTED ARTICLES ON INTERVIEWING

Arvey, Richard D. and James E. Campion. "The Employment Interview: A Summary and Review of Recent Research," *Personnel Psychology* 35 (1982): 281-322.

Baron, Robert A. "Interviewer's Moods and Reactions to Job Applicants: The Influence of Affective States on Applied Social Judgments," *Journal of Applied Social Psychology* 17 (October 1987): 911-926.

Campion, Michael A., Elliot D. Pursell, and Barbara K. Brown. "Structured Interviewing: Raising the Psychometric Properties of the Employment Interview," *Personnel Psychology* 41 (Spring 1988): 25-42.

Eder, Robert W. and Gerald R. Ferris, eds. *The Employment Interview*. Newbury Park, CA: Sage, 1989.

Fear, Richard. *The Evaluation Interview*, 4th edition. New York: McGraw-Hill, 1990.

Harris, Michael M. "Reconsidering the Employment Interview: A Review of Recent Literature and Suggestions for Future Research," *Personnel Psychology* 42 (Winter 1989): 691-726.

Jenks, James M. and Brian L.P. Zevnik. "The ABC's of Job Interviewing," *Harvard Business Review* 67 (July-August 1989): 38-42.

Rynes, Sara and Barry Gerhart. "Interviewer Assessments of Applicant 'Fit': An Exploratory Investigation." *Personnel Psychology* 43 (Spring 1990): 13-35.

Weston, David J. and Dennis L. Warmke. "Dispelling the Myths About Panel Interviews," *Personnel Administrator* (May 1988): 109-111.

EMPLOYMENT DISCRIMINATION

Equal Employment Opportunity Commission. *Technical Assistance Manual for the Americans with Disabilities Act.* Boston: Warren, Gorham and Lamont, 1992.

Ruthenglen, G. *Major Issues in the Federal Law of Employment Discrimination.* Washington, D.C.: Federal Judicial Center, 1987.

Uniform Guidelines on Employee Selection Procedures, Part 1607, Equal Employment Opportunity Commission. (1978) 29 CFR Ch.XIV.

RECRUITMENT

Josey, E.J. "E.J. Josey Recommends Recruitment Strategy," *Library Personnel News* 5 (1991): 6.

Heim, Kathleen. "Organizational Entry: Human Resources Selection and Adaptation in Response to a Complex Labor Pool," *Library Trends* 38 (Summer 1989): 21-31.

Mech, Terrence, "Recruitment and Selection of College Librarians," *Operations Handbook for the Small Academic Library*, edited by Gerard B. McCabe, Greenwood, 1989.

Moen, William E. and Kathleen M. Heim. *Librarians for the New Millennium.* Chicago: ALA, 1988.

Wright, Joyce C. "Recruitment and Retention of Minorities in Academic Libraries: A Plan of Action for the 1990s," *Illinois Libraries* 72 (November 1990): 621-625.

REFERENCE LETTERS

Bell, James D., James Castagnera, and Jane Patterson Young. "Employment References: Do You Know the Law?" *Personnel Journal* 63 (February 1984): 32-36.

Ryan, Ann Marie and Marja Lasek. "Negligent Hiring and Defamation: Areas of Liability Related to Pre-Employment Inquiries," *Personnel Psychology* 44 (1991): 293-319.

Wonder, Bruce D. and Kenneth S. Keleman. "Increasing the value of Reference Information," *Personnel Administrator* (March 1984): 98-103.

REJECTION LETTERS

Aamodt, Michael G. and Deborah L. Peggans. "Rejecting Applicants with Tact," *Personnel Administrator* (April 1988): 58-60.

SEARCH COMMITTEES

Fisher, William. "Use of Selection Committess by California Academic Libraries," *Journal of Academic Librarianship* 17 (November 1991): 276-283.

Harvey, John F. and Mary Parr. "University Library Search and Screen Committees," *College and Research Libraries* 37 (July 1976): 347-355.

Simpson, William A., "Why Search Committees Must Be Wary of Ex-Cavalry Officers, Condorcet's Paradox, and Dictators," *Research in Higher Education* 29 (1988): 149-159.

TRAINING

Creth, Sheila. *Effective On-the-Job Training.* Chicago: ALA, 1986.

Lipow, Anne Grodzins. "Why Training Doesn't Stick: Who Is to Blame," *Library Trends* 38 (Summer 1989): 62-72.

Noe, Raymond A. "Trainees' Attributes and Attitudes: Neglected Influences on Training Effectiveness," *Academy of Management Review* 11 (October 1986): 736-749.

INDEX

Dr. Rubin is Associate Professor at the School of Library and Information Science at Kent State University. Previously he served as Personnel Director of the Akron-Summit County Public Library in Akron, Ohio. He has written and spoken on the subject of human resource management for many years and is the author of the book, *Human Resource Management in Libraries: Theory and Practice* (Neal-Schuman, 1991).

Typography: Benchmark Production, Inc.
Cover: Apicella Design